Conflict and Resolution

Conflict
and
Resolution

Paul A. Mickey
and
Robert L. Wilson

abingdon press
Nashville   New York

CONFLICT AND RESOLUTION

Copyright © 1973 by Abingdon Press

Library of Congress Cataloging in Publication Data

Mickey, Paul A. 1937-   Conflict and resolution.
  1. Pastoral theology—Case studies. I. Wilson, Robert
Leroy, 1925-   joint author. II. Title.
BV4013.M5   253   73-4974

ISBN 0-687-09400-3

MANUFACTURED BY THE PARTHENON PRESS AT
NASHVILLE, TENNESSEE, UNITED STATES OF AMERICA

To the pastors and congregations whose lives
have been part of these studies in conflict

Contents

Introduction

Controversy and conflict are very much a part of everyone's life. Conflict may range from the tension between you and your next-door neighbor over his dog digging in your carefully manicured flower bed to the danger of all-out war in the Middle East.

Conflict seems to be increasing in our society. Whether or not this is actually the case, two other phenomena should be considered. First, the population of this planet is growing rapidly; there are simply more people to get into squabbles with their fellows. Even if the rate of conflict is not increasing, the total amount probably is. Second, technology has provided a system of almost instantaneous communications which brings events from every part of the globe into our living rooms. Thus, a bomb in Belfast or a riot in Rome will be graphically shown in living color on the six o'clock news. We are immediately aware of conflict anywhere in the world.

The church has something of a hard time with conflict, particularly conflict between individual Christians and between groups within the church itself. Controversy seems to be the very negation of much for which the church stands. It is seen as the opposite of reconciliation, as a force which separates people rather than bringing them together.

It is to be expected that there would be conflict outside the church. There would understandably be tensions between Christians and persons outside the church over a range of issues. But the existence of controversy inside the church is highly threatening, because for many people it implies weakness and failure of Christians to live up to the expectations of the gospel.

Differences between persons and groups do exist. People with the best of motives may pursue conflicting goals. Tension and controversy are the results. This occurs within the framework of the church. Because people feel strongly about religion, conflict within the church may be intense.

It is important for the church leader to recognize the presence of conflict and learn to deal with it constructively. The conflict situation, if handled in the proper way, may yield positive results. If the controversy is ignored or handled less skillfully, the situation may deteriorate, resulting in greater estrangement and even more severe conflict.

This is a book of case studies of conflict in the church. All the cases are authentic. They have been taken from actual situations in which the authors themselves or their associates have been directly involved. An attempt has been made to present the events exactly as they occurred. The real names of people and churches have not been used in order to permit the facts to be stated frankly.

A range of types of conflict in the church is the subject of these cases. Included will be situations in which there is conflict between the pastor and his people, between the congregation and the parent denomination, and between churches of different denominations.

Conflict between groups within the congregation will focus on such aspects as proposed church mergers and relocations and differences in program goals. One section will deal with conflicts among members of the church staff.

The use of the case method has several advantages. The reader begins with actual situations involving real people. The cases to be presented are from the parish, the place where people have contact with the Christian church. The reader discovers the theory or principle from the actual situation rather than by trying to find cases to fit a theory. Out of the specific incidents, he may develop not only a knowledge of how conflict occurs, but skill in handling situations himself when the need arises.

Although each case is relatively short, it will consist of three parts. These are:

1. *Background information.* The case will give enough background data to enable the reader to have a general understanding of the context in which the case is set.

2. *The conflict situation.* The case will focus on the specific event or series of events which has resulted in the conflict situation. This will be the major portion of each case.

3. *Point of decision.* The case will conclude at the point where some decision(s) on dealing with the conflict must be made. The case will not tell who did what, or how, or if the conflict was finally resolved.

At the conclusion of each case several questions for discussion will be given. These are designed to help the reader focus on the specific issues raised in the case and on the decisions which need to be made.

As the cases are analyzed, several general questions should be kept in mind. These include:

What are the factors causing the conflict?

Are there underlying factors which are different from the apparent causes of the controversy?

Who are the protagonists?

What were the critical points of decision which led to the present situation?

What options are available? What would be the probable result of each?

What relevance does the gospel have to this specific situation?

The authors are deeply indebted to the many laymen, pastors, and seminary students whose experiences are recounted on the following pages. It is our hope that these cases may help church leaders better understand conflict and channel it toward positive ends.

I   Conflict in the Church

Is conflict necessary in the church? How may we avoid conflict and still call people to repentance, redemption, and eternal life? Is it possible to understand conflict as a constructive experience? Does it enable us to perform the ministerial task of the church? These are some of the pressing questions as we consider the problem of "conflict in the church." In this chapter we want to suggest some guidelines for developing a constructive understanding of church conflict. There are four main areas in which we need to develop guidelines.

Chaos, Conflict, and Reconciliation— a Systematic Understanding

Our first task is to achieve an organized or systematic understanding of the nature of conflict. We experience a great deal of chaos in our lives and in the church, and we desperately want reconciliation. But we fear and avoid conflict. We cannot understand how experiencing or, worse yet, initiating conflict will move us toward love, mutual concern, and reconciliation.

We shy from open conflict in the church because we think of it as an end, and not a means to the end, of moving away from chaos, confusion, and suspicion toward love and reconciliation. Appropriately understood as a means to an end, conflict has to do with recognition, communication, and resolution of difficulties. Conflict, in this its proper sense, is not oriented ultimately toward upheaval and destruction but toward the constructive and reconciling resolution of disruptive and divisive forces.

Thus, the purpose of this chapter, and ultimately of the book, is to show that conflict is inseparably related to reconciliation *and* chaos. Chaos and reconciliation are related to each other like the North and South Poles, or the ends of a spectrum, or continuum. We cannot have one without the other because one is simply the opposite, or complementary side, of the other. So conflict connects chaos and reconciliation. It is a process which enables us to move from the one to the other.

Hence our thesis in this study: conflict occurs any time there is disturbance in the equilibrium and security of a protective environment. This may be an environment of religious beliefs, political thought, personality identity, group integrity, or nature itself. We want to show that conflict is a process and is neutral in itself, moving from chaos to reconciliation. It becomes valuable or threatening only as people experience its peculiar and redemptive way of joining the old and established to the new and not yet. Now, to expand this argument.

Chaos

Initially, change does not create reconciliation but introduces disruption and chaos. Any environment, with its security and protection, begins to disintegrate when new ways of doing things arc tried. For example, a congregation wants to construct a new sanctuary. A location

must be found on which to build. Once the building committee is ready to authorize the actual construction, the
first visible evidence of the new building is—what? It is
groundbreaking. Chaos. At the very heart of where the
group wants its new and beautiful sanctuary, ground is
broken and torn up. First the dignitaries come using a
hand shovel. Next the serious excavation begins with
bulldozers, and so forth. This relationship is also true if,
for example, one wants to build a snowman. The beautiful, soft, moist snow is disrupted. Footprints and a gap-
ing trench appear as the builder rolls his snowballs into
the sizes he wishes to represent the various parts of Mr.
Snowman's body. The front lawn or the field loses its
silky serenity because children or playful people wanted
to make a snowman. Finally, Mr. Snowman emerges.
He has a top hat, carrot nose, a pipe and scarf, and he is
stately. But his creators had to live with the chaos they
produced and conflict they felt about disrupting the land-
scape in order to create the snowman.

We must accept disruption and chaos in order to have
improvement and beauty. This movement from chaos to
reconciliation is true at all levels of life: building a new
sanctuary or a home, setting a broken bone, saving a
destructive marriage, or being converted spiritually. The
initial and necessary stage is chaos.

Reconciliation

Reconciliation and harmony are without doubt the
ultimate goals of the Christian life. We talk a lot about
reconciliation and grace, but there is the problem of

"cheap grace" and "cheap reconciliation." God's grace is not cheap. It comes through the cross and Jesus Christ. God reconciled us to himself through Christ, who knew our chaos and temptations. He participated fully in our lives. His life established the bond of sonship between the Father and us. Thus reconciliation is a matter of mutual recognition that a conflict is ended. Reconciliation is a goal but not the means to a goal.

Let's return to the illustration of Jesus. When the Gospel writers claim that Jesus became flesh and dwelt among us, they meant just that. Jesus did not reconcile continuously. He was not a "do-gooder." What if Jesus had reconciled himself to Satan during the wilderness temptation, or to Judas, or to the money changers, or to the crowds that wanted to make him a political hero? Reconciliation in that context would have been cheap, and disastrous. It would have destroyed God's goal (reconciliation), because the goal would have become the means, and man would not have been reconciled to God, who alone forgives sin. Jesus was not reconciled in the sense of accommodating; thus reconciliation was possible. In point of fact, Jesus stirred up conflict with Satan, Judas, the money changers, and the crowds.

Reconciliation is important. But it occurs only as a resolution of conflict. Conflict is anchored in *chaos* and *reconciliation*.

Conflict

Conflict is a process; it is a means to an end. It connects the disruption (chaos) of the old and established to the harmony (resolution) of the new and not yet reconciled. Thus we are suspicious. Must we have conflict to change things? Perhaps there should be a better way, but there is not. So conflict is central to Christian experience and doctrine.

All movement and change involve conflict: beliefs, personal identity, behavior patterns, attitudes, church expansions, preaching, missionary work, Sunday school lessons, staff relations, and so forth. The experience of conflict is not limited to political ideology, racial tensions, or student confrontations. Indeed, one could argue that much of our intense awareness of conflict in politics, race, and student relations emerges out of poor and inadequate understanding of conflict. We fail to acknowledge this connection between chaos and reconciliation in every change.

The church should be able to accept and affirm this truth more readily than the general public. The Gospels witness to Jesus' fulfilling the law to establish a new order. Throughout his ministry, conflict was involved. The supreme example was Jesus' outright conflict with his contemporaries, which ended with his execution on the cross as a criminal.

Conflict is not an end in itself. Rather, it is a means to an end. And the purpose of this book is to illustrate the close relation between conflict and reconciliation through the use of actual case studies. Thus the churchmen can become aware of the nature of conflict and how it works in their lives.

Conflict is present and necessary in our lives because

our lives involve change; and no change, as we have argued, occurs without this movement *from* chaos and disorganization *to* resolution and reconciliation. Conflict is a part-process. That is, it is central in the life of the church. But it is neither the substance nor the goal of the church. It is inseparable from the direction and goals of the church, but it remains a part-process. Our goal here is to present conflict as real but not as final.

Conflict: Birthright of the Church— a Theological Understanding

Is conflict a theological category? Yes, it is. It is, as we mentioned earlier, not a final category but a means category. Consider this illustration. Many commentators and people in the church claim they have never seen the church at large so demoralized. Membership is down. Theology is ridiculed. Beliefs ignored. Sensitivities abused. Finances misused. Ministers ignorant. Laymen angry. Leadership divided. The list could go on. Part of the frustration and grievance stems from the technological and psychological age in which we find ourselves. If something goes wrong with our bank account or if the store bills us incorrectly, it's the computer's fault! No *person* openly takes responsibility for much of anything. Computer technology has become both *a* cause and *the* scapegoat for too much that goes on in commerce. But that's hardly the full story.

Another side to this picture is the "psychological" or

"thereapeutic" man. This means that as individuals we develop uncanny ways of psychologizing away everything. All relationships may be understood fully from a psychological perspective, we believe. Thus we all are participating in a "collapse of the transcendent." [1] For example, children talk back to their parents because they learn from Sigmund Freud that parents are only little children grown larger. No one dares to believe advertising or guarantees. The annual financial statements from churches and other businesses are intended to conceal not reveal. Sermons tend to deal with "adjustment problems"; they are thin on biblical content, and God is not supposed to look like a grandfather. The war in Vietnam continued despite public promises of three Presidents.

In effect, we have lost the assurance and credibility of the transcendent. This occurs when we lose sight of the means category of conflict in theology. We want the final category of reconciliation without the means—and so we have it. We have no conflict. Of course we cannot think of God as a grandfather-type figure with a silvery beard. Of course children dismiss their parents as overgrown and outdated infants. Of course church groups cannot admit their budgets don't balance. Of course the seminary-trained minister has all the answers. Of course we have no sin, it's simply our hang-ups. We deny that we have conflict over what our image of God should be, or who mature parents are, or what the fiscal responsibil-

[1] Peter Homans, *Theology After Freud* (Indianapolis: Bobbs-Merrill, 1970), especially chapter 6, "Transcendence, Mass Culture, and the Psychology of Distance: An Interpretation."

ity of church leaders is, or whether recent seminary grad-
uates have theological integrity. Our negative self-feel-
ings jump, conveniently, comfortably, and desperately
toward reconciliation and resolution. We leap to final
categories but deny and ignore the means to those ends.

Sam Keen points out in *To a Dancing God* that we
have lost confidence in the transcendent. Thus we can do
whatever we want to because we don't feel guilty about
it. But in this magnificent discovery we have been caught,
theologically, selling our souls to the devil; we have lost
the capacity for wonder.[2]

We cannot experience wonder and majesty when the
church is hell-bent on cheap reconciliation and a denial
of conflict in witness. True wonder, respect, and guilt
come only as we begin to reestablish the means category
of *conflict* which connects the final categories of transcendence and immanence, parent and child, education
and inspiration, accountability and credibility. We simply
cannot have the final category of chaos. Conflict simply
ties together. It is not the instigator; it is the means to
reconciliation. The shortest distance between two points
is not always a straight line. Assassination attempts on
public figures in the United States during the past ten
years suggest the lunacy of employing that principle to
achieve political reconciliation and resolution.

Conflict is a profoundly important theological category, albeit subordinated to the final categories. Jesus as

[2] Sam Keen, *To a Dancing God* (New York: Harper & Row,
1970). See also his earlier exploration, *Apology for Wonder* (Harper
& Row, 1969).

we know, used conflict as a basic element in his ministry. For example, in John 8:1-8, well-intending righteous people were going to stone a woman who had been caught in adultery. Jesus asked them to reflect, for just a moment, on their own behavior before stoning her. None of the accusers tossed even a pebble. Why? Jesus raised some conflict for them. Were they, in fact, displacing their own guilt feeling about transgressing the law (and not necessarily the law regarding adultery) and projecting this onto this woman? Was she to bear the burdens of *their* sins while they, the righteous, could feel even more righteous? Elsewhere Jesus asked us to remove the log in our own eye before performing surgery for a speck in someone else's eye.

The point of all this is to show how Jesus used the case study method in his own ministry: he asked his flock to examine their own behavior and motives and to consider at least two sides of the story. The cases which we have prepared cover a broad range of interactions and situations. In them we ask of the reader the same kind of thing Jesus asks of all of us who seek to do his will.

Conflict is a hallmark of the church, and its birthmark. It is inescapable. Conflict is an appropriate theological category. It is a means category connecting the final categories of reconciliation and chaos. Also we note that Jesus employed conflict as a means in his ministry. Thus, both in principle and practice we have authority in theology to reintroduce conflict as an integral part of Christian ministry. Therefore we need to recover and accept conflict as a necessary part of the church's concern to revitalize and save itself, its ministry, and mankind.

Conflict and Resolution in the Parish— a Dynamic Understanding

Conflict is the part-process. It is the means connecting chaos and reconciliation. On a practical level conflict is dynamic. We use "dynamic" here in the sense the Greeks used it. It is the relationship between the tensions and equilibriums of various energy forms or forces. And in the parish our dynamic understanding of conflict means that life is far from being understood through analysis of surface behavior alone.

We are presenting cases that deal with explicit conflicts. They range from faith differences to difficulties with denominational representatives. Our purpose is to acquaint the reader with the diversity of situations in which the potential for conflict is part of the character of that situation itself. Too often we dismiss conflict by saying something like, "Well, it's just a personality difference between us." Or, "He (or that group) is so stupid he'll never understand." Or, "They lack the vision the church should have," and so forth. Our point is that it is not that simple! What emerges on the surface is dynamically related to feelings and conflicts that are far removed from appearance. But they need to be considered nonetheless. For example, Mr. Brown is a senior high counselor who "attacks" the other youth counselor (Mr.

George) for recently taking the church young people on a trip to the beach. Brown is convinced that such secular activities expose the Christian to the demonic forces of the world. But, we discover after his tongue-lashing, Mr. Brown, who is in charge of this particular Sunday's youth meeting, devotes the entire two-hour program to a softball game. Is there not some conflict between his sermon and the fact that his leadership consists of a recreation program?

On the surface it appears that Mr. Brown is against worldly entertainment and wants good, solid, spiritual youth programs. But is this all that he is communicating to Mr. George and the youth? Further analysis might reveal several levels of conflict between Mr. Brown's statements and his behavior. What are those conflicts? Why do they exist?

There are a number of dynamic possibilities. First, consider Brown's negative reaction to the beach trip. Why is he afraid the youth will be corrupted? Did that once happen to him, so now he is very sensitive to the problem? Was he angry because he wasn't included? And why wasn't he? There are numerous possibilities why Mr. Brown is so against the beach trip. Likewise, why does he settle for a recreation program whereas he has talked about the positive need for spiritual growth? Consider some of the possible levels of conflict here. Brown is interested in engaging the youth in serious consideration of spiritual problems, but has he difficulty in expressing himself, so the youth tend to laugh at him? If they have laughed, and that now scares him away from this kind of discussion, why did they laugh? It certainly was not because Mr. Brown fancies himself a spiritual comedian. Was he getting too close to home with the youth? Or does he talk a big line about spirituality but really never deliver on anything more serious than recreational projects?

These are simply a few suggestions about the levels of conflict that may be involved in this brief encounter between Mr. Brown and Mr. George over good youth programs. These various levels need thoughtful analysis so that the true character and potential beneath the surface of the conversation or encounter may be recognized. This would help Mr. Brown, Mr. George, and the youth come to a more open understanding of their real *expectations, values,* and *differences in perception* about the group and what it should be doing.

Sometimes the conflict between what one says and does is rather obvious, as in Brown's case. In other instances the dynamics are extremely subtle. One may not readily observe conflict, discrepancy, and contradiction between what is said and meant, or what is said and done, or what is said and the expected response. What goes on between these various levels of saying and doing, expectation and response, and context constitute the *dynamics.* And we need to develop an understanding of these relationships and how they may be altered and what effect changing one level or dimension of the dynamics may have upon other components.

As we have suggested in the case of Mr. Brown, the apparent conflict between what he says and does may be a smoke screen for some underlying motives which he may or may not sense himself. Thus, the case studies in this volume are designed to enhance the reader's sensitivities to the tension (dynamics) between the various levels of communication and meaning in encounters.

What kinds of conflict or tension may be involved in a given encounter? There are basically four. One is *confusion*. One party does not fully grasp the problem itself. As a result he may be confused in his analysis and statement of the problem as well as in considering workable alternatives. He may be uncertain of the problem, but he is certain that something is wrong. Or, at least, he doesn't feel comfortable with what is going on, whether he can name it or not.

Another kind of conflict is *communication*. There may be conflict introduced through physical breakdown in communication. For example, Jim and Joe are so out of sorts with each other that when Jim speaks, Joe does not hear because he has developed a nonlistening habit. Joe literally cannot recall what was said because he was preoccupied with preparing a defense or response of his own. Physical breakdown in communication is present any time there is a lot of conflict between parties. A second type of communication conflict is a breakdown in personal communication. This kind of problem arises when there is doubt or ambiguity about a communication which may have two or more possible meanings. In this case the "receiver" party (Joe) tries to clarify the meaning by asking the "sender" party (Jim) if what he hears is what was sent: for example, "I hear you saying . . ."

A third kind of conflict is the *put on*. Here party A takes the initiative to overstate a problem or his involvement in it. Either positive or negative involvement is presented so dramatically that the statement appears entirely believable. It has the added ring of truth because A suggests that his own integrity is deeply involved. So how could party B dare to conclude otherwise? The conflict arises because B really has no hard evidence to contradict both the literal and moral implications of the case as stated by A.

For example, a men's group for years has sponsored an annual Christmas party for some children whose families are on welfare in the town in which Zion Church is located. But this past year several civic groups have taken up a similar project. The welfare case workers feel the men's group should shift their project to another area of the children's welfare (an evening and Saturday tutorial program was suggested) to avoid a duplication of services. In point of fact, the Christmas party is easier to administer than the tutorial program. But the president (Mr. Bigheart) of the Zion's Men's Group delivers a diatribe in the administrative board meeting against this proposed shift. He lists in great detail the merits and meaning of this long-standing project. What other members of the board, who are about to be convinced by this speech to oppose the welfare department and support the men's club, don't know is that, through ingenious bookkeeping, Mr. Bigheart has been claiming the expenses incidental to the party as a personal donation to charity for tax purposes. For reasons now obvious to the reader but not to the members of the board, Mr. Bigheart's impassioned speech is a *put on*. Very much conflict is being introduced by his telling it all, but not saying all there is to be said.

A fourth kind of conflict is the *lure*. The most common example would be the high-pressure car salesman. A prospective buyer's attention is riveted to all the accessories of the car. The style, color, or whatever seems appealing to his immediate attention is highlighted by the salesman. But what, of course, is not said is very, very important. What are the time-payment charges, the actual trade-in value of the old jalopy, and so on? So we have the *lure,* or the "one-two punch." The attention of the customer is affixed or transfixed on certain obvious details. The fact that these are not the most important details in the transaction is obscured. So the "one" punch (the accessories are discussed in great detail) is fielded nicely. But watch out for the "two" punch. Or, in other words, "Why didn't you watch out for the haymaker?" It's too late once the real blow has been delivered.

As one readily observes from these four kinds of conflict, the more one denies that conflicts and tensions exist, the more deeply he becomes bound by them. Thus, avoidance or denial of conflict is the least favorable resolution. It is ultimately the most painful and expensive way of responding to a situation. So, understanding that there are several kinds of conflict is only half the battle. How is one to increase his understanding so he can do something about resolving the felt conflicts and reconciling the problem itself?

Oddly enough, we may take our lead from Saul Alinsky, whose career was oriented toward enabling people to deal with conflict constructively. Mr. Alinsky's approach was to introduce conflict in order to accomplish the political goals of enabling our democratic society to be democratic for all its people. Let us consider his three rules of power: (1) "Power is not only what you have but what the enemy thinks you have." (2) "Never go outside the experience of your people." (3) "Wherever possible go outside of the experience of the enemy." [3] Alinsky was concerned with social injustices and grievances. And he was concerned pragmatically with enabling the have-nots to take from the haves by heightening the conflict between them. These three principles are the backbone of his philosophy.

The church is interested ultimately in reconciliation. But conflict must necessarily be experienced first as a means toward that final end. So we have to revise Alinsky's principles of power politics to move beyond conflict to reconciliation. Hence, our responsibility is to make the experience of our people and the enemy *congruent*. We learn to speak from the same experience and understanding, and to respect our relative strengths and power. We move beyond the conflicts of *confusion, communication breakdown, put on,* and *lure.* We want to establish clarity of thought, commonality in meaning, honesty in programs, and respect for the integrity of the other.

[3] Saul Alinsky, *Rules for Radicals* (New York: Random House, 1971), p. 127.

Thus, as we attempt to gain a dynamic understanding of conflict, we go beyond Alinsky and use his principles of power as he used them—to heighten conflict. But we use them to resolve conflict by moving in the opposite direction. That is, we move toward commonality and reconciliation. Here we have tried to stress the need for a dynamic understanding of conflict. And again we underscore the importance of realizing that reconciliation does not occur without conflict. It is possible, through an appropriate understanding of conflict and relational dynamics, to move through manifest conflict toward final reconciliation.

Conflict as Power for Pastoral Ministry— Ministerial Understanding

We have talked about conflict as a disruption of the equilibrium of a protective environment, whatever it may be. We have mentioned the need for a theological understanding of and appreciation for conflict. For example, consider the conflict of the transcendent and immanent in life. Thirdly, we have analyzed various components of conflict in moving from chaos through conflict to reconciliation. Now we need to be concerned about the appropriate use of conflict as a source of power in the parish context. Again, let us turn to Mr. Alinsky and one of his principles. But we rewrite it in the ministerial context. He talked about getting conditions changed and saw the major responsibility of the organizer as creating issues. Issues, in contrast to a bad scene, are something *you* think *you* can do something about. Once an issue is created, then negotiation about resolution of that issue commences. Negotiation occurs because both parties have the power to compel negotiation.[4]

Alinsky's overall concern was to move people from inaction, apathy, and resignation to focus on specific issues. Once people take hold of specific issues, they have the power to do something about it (the bad scene). They can compel negotiation because both parties know the have-not group has a hold on a serious problem which neither party may ignore.

The purpose of this book, quite frankly, is to help people in the church. They may be pastors, laymen, seminary students, denominational executives, or bishops. But they all need to be able to get hold of *specific* issues. Look at the various chapter headings. They represent issues which the specific cases illustrate in a detailed, concrete manner. Thus this book provides specific cases to illustrate the specific issues now before the church. Careful analysis and discussion of the specific cases will enable a group to achieve a focus on an issue and thereby gain the power of insight so as to compel negotiation.

Let us look at what we call *negotiation*. Negotiation points us toward the goal in a conflict situation. It is directly related to power. Now power is the method, or the "how", of negotiation. These two, negotiation and power, are interwoven and inseparable. But we will separate them briefly for purposes of discussion.

[4] *Ibid.,* p. 119.

Negotiation comes from the Latin *negotior*—to do business, to carry on business. That is, negotiation is not related to concession or dominance and submission. Rather, it is related to conducting business and taking the parties and issues involved in those affairs seriously. Negotiation facilitates business; it does not do away with it. So the goal of organizing around specific issues, in a "bad scene," is not to disrupt commerce but to enhance it. By compelling others to take specific problems seriously, a reasonable integration is possible.

And this is where power, the corollary of negotiation, comes in. It goes almost without saying that one cannot compel business to be done if there is no business left to do. So we must remember this fundamental truth when we discuss power as a method for compelling. So many who cry "Power to the people" are not interested in compelling men to do business or to engage in commerce. They are interested in disruption and destruction only. But that is a nihilistic understanding of power and not what Alinsky meant. Nor is it what we mean. Power is simply an aggregate of feelings and convictions brought to bear on a specific issue and expressed in such a way that successful negotiations are both necessary and possible.

So it is; conflict is directly related to power and negotiation in the church. It enables us to move beyond apathy, complacency, and feelings of powerlessness. It provides a focus on specific issues. It allows us to enter into negotiation and, ultimately, to move toward resolution and reconciliation.

Many of the problems the church faces now were not seen as issues twenty years ago, or even ten. Our problems are diverse, and our society is increasingly pluralistic. The parish seems inundated with problems to the point of being a bad scene. A general feeling of demoralization, apathy, and powerlessness permeates. The church has power, a tremendous potential for power. But the regaining of power and its use to compel negotiation with the sins of personal transgression and social evil can only come with the ability to identify issues and make "something bad" a particular problem.

This book and these cases are offered with the hope that they will contribute to the church's regaining its power. If groups of concerned churchmen will take the time and effort to look closely at specific issues and particular problems, they can chart a course of action. The value of this volume is that these cases, while actual case histories in point of fact, have been prepared in such a way that any group can analyze them and begin to make connections between what happened in "that case" and what is happening "in our case."

Our purpose in preparing this book was not to present a collection of stories. We want to enable the church, as a group of people who often feel very much a part of the have-nots, to gain personal, spiritual, sociological, and political power to bring about the kingdom of God on earth.

We cannot play church. We have to do business. We have to negotiate because those outside the church are negotiating with us. If people are to reject us and turn away from the church of Jesus Christ, then it should be because of negotiation. From a common ground we simply cannot agree! The last thing we want is for people to become reconciled to the church in a negative way. That is, we do not want the church rejected because it did not have the power to compel others or itself to negotiate the faith. We have to take seriously particular problems: personal salvation, social action, group integrity, church staff relations, whatever. This book is designed to help us go beyond play and apathy: to negotiate; to identify problems; to come clean on where we stand on specific problems. We need to rediscover power in the church.

Conclusion

So chaos, apathy, anger, confusion, and doubt are the starting points. Our need is to generate conflict as a response to apathy and doubt. We cannot simply bleed them off in order to neglect and ignore them. Rather we want to enable people, inside and outside the church, to move beyond the impinging enclosures of chaos, to move toward the possibilities and the risks required for reconciliation in our situation. Conflict as expressed in the sense of the power to compel others to listen is necessarily part of the desired process. It is the connective between frustration and abandonment and reconciliation and resolution.

The cases we present are illustrations of conflict. But

they are not intended to entertain or to be course material for a graduate class in Monday-morning quarterbacking. Rather, these cases are intended to enable and encourage the readers to empathize with the situations and then begin to come to terms with the specific issues involved. Thus real quarterbacks and leaders are made: they are acquainted with the game and with specific strategies for confronting specific problems in their situation; they compel negotiation with specific persons, groups, ideas, and organizations. Our purpose is to discover anew the common ground and common experience to move toward the ultimate and final goal of the church: being reconciled to God the Father.

II Facing Personal Conflict

Each person is an individual. Each group of which a person is a member has its individuality. We may applaud or lament changes in our beliefs, our feelings about ourselves and others, or our group membership. But what is constant and inevitable in all relationships is some degree of personal conflict. Whenever personal or group individuality is expressed, conflict of some kind results because differences have become clear and recognizable. In this sense, personal conflict is seen as neither good nor bad. But it is inevitable and inherently part of our personal and group individuality.

The Christian needs to learn to accept conflict in all his relations, not passively hoping to make it go away, but actively working to clarify it. Briefly, there are three kinds or levels of personal conflict: intrapersonal, interpersonal, and group.

Intrapersonal

This refers to conflict which occurs inside us, usually taking one of two forms. A problem is either someone else's fault or it's my fault. In the first form we engage in projection or externalization of the conflict. When something goes wrong, we lay the fault with our husband or wife, son or daughter, preacher or president. We don't take responsibility for what may have actually happened because we feel that the cause is outside our control.

The conflict is resolved by projecting both the cause and effect outside ourselves.

The opposite dynamic is equally powerful in resolving internal conflict; in this case we assume responsibility for everything so that we always feel guilty when husband or wife, son or daughter, preacher or president does something wrong. We see ourselves failing to do this or that; we become despondent and feel worthless. The problem here is that the intrapersonal conflict is resolved by turning it inward upon ourselves and punishing our "self"—whether we deserve it or not. We have, in point of fact, resolved the conflict but at considerable price both for ourselves and others.

Generally, intrapersonal conflict tends to be resolved either by taking more responsibility than we should or less responsibility than we should for things which go wrong. We tend to either internalize (keep it within) or externalize (thrust it upon someone else) our conflict as a way of achieving a premature resolution.

Interpersonal

This involves transactions with others. A typical form of conflict, for example, is Jill, who feels she cannot hold her own with Marge, who wants very much for Jill to be more open and engaging. Other people, Marge in this case, are a threat to Jill. What Marge says or does, or when she is simply around, makes Jill uneasy and vulnerable to say and do "dumb" things. This is a defensive or "holding action" conflict. There are certain people who make us feel uncomfortable and in whose presence we have great difficulty being ourselves.

A second type of interpersonal conflict is related to our need to improve our relations and to engage in expansive or expressive experiences in which we find joy and satisfaction. This involves conflict in going beyond the status quo. For example, it is often very difficult for a husband and wife to complement each other in terms of the positive effect one has upon the other. To tell a spouse, "When you do such-and-such, it makes me feel good," raises so much conflict that generally we just don't get it said. This is not a matter of being threatened or intimidated by another; rather, it is a conflict over moving toward openness and new satisfactions in interpersonal relations.

Thus our interpersonal relations are a constant source of conflict in both defensive and expressive ways.

Group

In group relations we tend to identify positively with the group of which we are a member and to perceive other groups with disinterest, bewilderment, or antagonism. Our group may be the minority group, but we feel it is "right." We see this at work in the plea that while Christianity represents a minority of the world population, it is right. The sense of our group being right is all the more likely if ours is a majority group. Personally, we need and must have groups with which we can identify positively. We are able to deal with intrapersonal and interpersonal conflicts more easily if we find ourselves in a group of people who are basically compatible and who help us resolve our conflicts in the context of the group by providing group support.

Correspondingly, what may not have been a conflict for us personally becomes one as a result of our group's sense of conflict. This is transferred to us. Now we feel it and want the group, with our support, to resolve that conflict. Generally the action takes the form of wanting to throw those rascals (them) out and put in the good guys (us). In group conflict we tend to dismiss the other group(s) by admitting we don't "dig" them, or we will stereotype them as hippie, whitey, honkey, radical, communist, Bircher, and so on. So our conflicts are not just internal to us but are related very deeply to other persons and groups.

Whatever else may be said, and however we may diagnose the source of human behavior, we must affirm that conflict is an inevitable part of our lives intrapersonal, interpersonal, and group; thereby we begin to recognize it more clearly, manage it more constructively, and live more creatively.

Thanks for Listening

Carl Davis is a seminary student who has had some training in relating to people with personal conflicts and in trying to help them confront, manage, and relate constructively to painful conflicts. Of the conversation he reports, he comments that it represents about half of what was actually said. But he feels enough is presented to give us a feel for what went on.

Recently I was walking back to the Residence Hall after lunch. It was a beautiful day. I noticed a girl I knew sitting off in the woods by herself. I sensed, even from a distance, that she was there for reasons other than just to enjoy the day. My relationship to this girl has been that she is a close friend of a girl that I date. She is a very happy-go-lucky girl, always the life of the party. I debated with myself for several seconds whether to let her know that I was even aware of her (she was across the street and back in the woods, so it would have been easy not to be). I finally decided to walk over to her and see if I could find out what was going on—just sort of play it by ear and see what happened. I was uninvited.

Carl: What's the matter?

Peggy: Everything! (tears in her eyes)

Carl: It's really that bad, huh? (sat down beside her)

Peggy: Yes . . . (long pause) I bet you didn't think I could cry—the girl that's always laughing. I can't tell you about it.

Carl: O.K.

Peggy: (After long pause) How are you supposed to counsel a person who doesn't want to talk . . . just sit there?

Carl: If that's what they want, but I didn't come over—to "counsel" you. Would you rather be left alone?

Peggy: There is no point in you being uncomfortable because I'm not talking.

Carl: I'm not uncomfortable, but if you'd rather be alone, I'll leave.

Peggy: If it doesn't bother you, you can stay.
(We sat in silence for ten or fifteen minutes as she continued to cry—the tears just kept filling her eyes. After she had stopped crying and staring at the ground, she began to look up and observe what was happening around her—people walking by, etc.)

Carl: Let's go for a walk before we get a cold from sitting on this rock.

Peggy: O.K. (walked for several minutes) I just wish I could get mad instead of being so hurt.

Carl: Why don't you go ahead and get mad?!

Peggy: Because I don't know whether to be mad at the other person or myself.

Carl: If you want someone to be mad at, you can get mad at me for interrupting your privacy.

Peggy: (Laughs a little) No . . . I don't want to do that. Besides, that wouldn't do any good.

Carl: It might at least give you a chance to get some things out.

Peggy: Maybe so. (walked in silence for several minutes)

Carl: What is it that makes this other person so important to you?

Peggy: We were planning on getting married. Is that enough of a reason?

Carl: Yes, it sure is! (walked on in silence) Do you think that the things he said were true?

Peggy: I don't know . . . I need to talk to him. I know I'm being evasive, but I can't talk about it.

Carl: I don't want you to think that you have to. (walked on in silence)

Peggy: It sure doesn't do much for my self-esteem . . . absolutely zero!

Carl: Well, I know some people who do think a lot of you, and I do, too!

Peggy: (Smiling) Thanks. (walked on in silence) It's really bad when you have an ugly-duckling complex for twenty-one years, and just when you really start to feel beautiful, someone tells you that you *are* an ugly duckling.

Carl: Especially when it's someone close to you . . .

Peggy: Yes. (came to an intersection)

Carl: Which way do you want to go?

Peggy: Back to the dorm, I guess.

Carl: Are you ready for that yet?

Peggy: Yes . . . I am. (assuringly) Thanks.

Carl demonstrates unusual patience and restraint at many points in this conversation to allow Peggy to begin to accept her own feelings and then begin to share them with him. Peggy's feelings about herself seem to move beyond the deep hurt and rejection which she must have felt resulting from the broken relationship with her fiancé. Both her interpersonal relations and her self-image have suffered.

Questions for Discussion

How do you feel Carl handled the situation? Would you have wanted him, or yourself, to have related to Peggy differently? What do you think was going on inside Peggy during this extended conversation? Do we show this kind of sensitivity in our church relations? Would you want Carl for your pastor? Why?

Are All Kids Like This?

Allen Goodfellow is a young layman who has volunteered to teach a junior high church school class Sunday mornings. He presents the following both from the point of view of what was happening to him and in relation to the class. His is not a casual interpersonal or group conflict.

This Sunday school class is made up of the most difficult group of youngsters I have ever dealt with. In conjunction with the pastor (with whom the kids will have nothing to do), I have decided this is due to their social environment. They all come from poor white families. With the exception of about two out of the eight kids involved, the families are characterized by drinking fathers, neurotic mothers, and adultery on both sides.

From the first it was suggested to me by the pastor not to expect anything from these kids. He suggested that I just be with them. In this process of being with them, however, I have experienced what I consider to be four stages:

1. First was the "good guy" stage. Here I tried to be one of them. I thought that by talking their language, I could work from inside to help them. But instead this only merged into stage two.

2. The "sucker" stage. At this point the kids were really taking advantage of me, my car, and my money. Sunday school class was a madhouse, and our social activities away from the church were only chances to sneak away and be with boys. This led to stage three, where I finally gave vent to my indignation.

3. The utter frustration stage. At this point I simply gave up on trying to be nice. I came to believe that I had exercised too much restraint and that now was the time for power. Going through the fiery flame of this stage led finally to the last stage.

4. The "struggling-along-and-slowly-getting-somewhere" stage. They now know that I care for them, but also that I mean business.

The encounter that follows took place distinctly at the beginning of stage three. I went to class that Sunday with the idea that for once I was going to get a complete Sunday school lesson taught.

Allen: This morning our lesson is going to be on the meaning of worship. (With this beginning, two people were listening, while there were three pairs of conversations going on among the others. I could detect that two of the girls, Linda and Darlene, were talking about a boy.) Linda, how would you define worship?

Linda: Huh? Uh. I don't know. Going to church, I guess.

Allen: Yeah. That's right to a certain extent. (Meanwhile two other girls, Jane and Alice, are talking about another boy. George and Henry are beginning to act up at the back of the room.) Jane, how would you define worship?

Jane: I don't know. (turns to continue talking to Alice)

Allen: Bill (one of those who was listening), how would you define worship?

Bill: Gathering at church in order to praise God. (At this point the others were talking so loud that I could hardly hear. I decided to try to make some point of contact.)

Allen: Yeah. That's good, Bill. (then loudly in order to break their conversation) Linda, Jane, do you think that your friends or boyfriends at school would want to come to our church?

Linda: No! And what difference does it make anyway? What do our boyfriends have to do with the lesson?

Darlene: Yeah. You always try to talk about different things. We never learn anything because you don't stick to the lesson.

Allen: Now wait just a minute. I try every week to teach you the lesson. But you're always talking so much that the only way I can get to you is to try and enter into what you are talking about. (At this point one of the girls, Alice, was hitting one of the boys.) Alice, I better not see you do that again.

Linda: (In a very nasty tone) What are you getting her for? You never say anything to the boys. (At about that moment, George threw a spitball and hit Linda on the face.)

Allen: George (yes, I'm shouting here), if I ever see you throw another spitball in this class, you're either going to walk out that door yourself, or I'm going to put you out. Now either you sit down and be quiet, or get out. (turning back to Linda) And you better not talk to me in that tone again. If you don't like what I do here, you don't have to come. (They all sat in silence for a moment, kind of wide-eyed, knowing I was serious in what I was saying. Finally one of the girls who listens spoke up.)

Martha: If Linda's or George's mamma found out how they had been acting up, they sure would get whippings.

Allen: (Speaking to the whole class) Well, I'm sure all of your parents would be upset if they thought you cut up in church, but you don't have to worry about me telling on you. The point is that you all are going to start listening, or you don't get to come. We come to church to learn about ourselves, about Christ, and about God; and that's exactly what we're going to do from now on. (I estimate that this encounter took about fifteen minutes. For the thirty minutes more of the class, they sat still and listened, surprisingly, not seeming to resent doing so.)

If you are looking for confrontation, here it is. It is helpful for us to have Allen's preliminary words to give us some sense of where he saw himself in the midst of this and what was happening. Thus, the strong and abrasive interaction between him and the class could be somewhat anticipated.

Questions for Discussion

How do we feel about Allen's use of power in this encounter? Are we tempted to say "Right on," or would we advocate a more restrained way of coping? What is your impression of the youth, especially Linda and Jane? What are their personal conflicts which are brought to and expressed in Sunday school class? Is this kind of abrasive encounter appropriate in Sunday school? Why or why not?

I've Had It

John Williams shares a situation in which a couple is in the midst of some serious conflict; their personal relations seem quite congenial and supportive. But their intrapersonal conflict, especially Ted's, tends to find expression in feelings of worthlessness and inadequacy. There is very little projection as might be expressed by the phrase, "but why me?"

This case involves me and Ted and Henrietta Brown, a couple in their mid-forties who are members of a church I served as pastor prior to last June. They are the parents of a fourteen-year-old son and two married daughters.

During the past three and a half years they have seen many changes in their lives, including several traumatic experiences. Just recently Ted has learned that an old head injury has now permanently affected the motor coordination in his left leg. Also, he is having to get out of a business partnership at great financial loss. Henrietta works as a secretary in a local insurance office and fears that she will have to bear the major burden of their support. These two blows follow three other very traumatic experiences in a rather unstable home situation.

I had been their pastor through their troubles, helping them and sharing these difficulties with them. Henrietta had been the choir director and organist for awhile. She has resigned as choir director but continued to play for the evening services. Ted has been superintendent of the church school and was the chairman of the administrative board when I left.

On a recent trip back for a funeral, I phoned Henrietta (I couldn't reach Ted) just to give my regards to them both before heading home.

Henrietta: Oh, John, your calling is like an answer to prayer!

John: I've wondered how you all have been.

Henrietta: John, I'm worried about Ted. He seems to be lost and defeated. I don't know what we are going to do. If only you were here; we need to talk with you. Somehow we've been unable to talk with Tom. (Tom is the present pastor. I learned that Ted had gone to the church to see him the previous week and lost his nerve. Also, the Saturday before, Henrietta while exercising on her bicycle had ridden by the church several times without being able to go in.)

John: Henrietta, I called because I hated to leave without speaking to you. We must be on our way back, but we'll detour through Springside and stop for a cup of coffee.

Henrietta: I'll leave work now and go on home and find Ted—we'll be waiting for you. (On arriving in Springside, I left my wife at the home of friends, and I went on to the Browns'.)

Ted: John, I've had it. I just don't know what to do. I can't seem to get hold of myself. No job, and I don't know whether I can hold one if I get it.

John: I could call George Carter, a clergyman who has specialized in counseling. Ted, will you go to see him? Will you ask your pastor to go with you?

Ted: If you think it would help. What could he do?

John: George Carter is assigned to the county mental health center, and is available to counsel anyone in the denomination. He's done some marvelous work coordinating the various agencies that offer help in various areas. He would talk with you. Possibly give you some tests, maybe send you to the rehabilitation office for job training or further education; and hopefully you will regain some confidence in your ability and receive training in an area suitable for you.

Ted: I'll try anything that you think will help. (He's obviously close to breaking down at this point and excuses himself to go to the bathroom.)

Henrietta: (While Ted is out of the room) John, is Ted capable of getting and holding a job? Has he lost all of his ability? Oh, I don't know what to do, and I feel so inadequate, so helpless. I feel like I've failed him.

John: Henrietta, Ted has shown in the past that he has ability and that he is capable of doing a good job, in fact, of running a business profitably and efficiently. Probably he needs your love and support just now more than he has ever needed you, for as you know, he adores you and that's quite something after all your years together. He's honest, kind, and completely faithful to you and the children. (Ted returns and apparently has overheard some of the conversation.)

Ted: I've wondered if everything has affected my

mind. (Henrietta chimes in with agreement)
I'm not sure of anything.

John: Ted, you too, Henrietta, listen to me. Everyone who sees a counselor or goes for help
at a mental health center is not suffering
from a mental disorder—often not even
from an emotional disorder. Most often, because of varying circumstances beyond their
control, they simply cannot cope with their
problems. Getting help from a competent,
experienced source is the logical, rational
thing to do so that they can cope with all
that life has dealt them. I'd help in a minute
if I were going to be here, but these people
have more to offer than I have, and I would
ask you to go even if I were here.

Henrietta: Maybe I need to go too. I'm sure I need
help.

John: Yes, Henrietta, I think it would be good for
you to go, but I think they will ask Ted to
bring you at the proper time.

Henrietta: This looks like the best thing to do.

Ted: Yes, I'm glad you were able to come by.
Sorry about Dr. James—so many things
have changed—but I'm glad you're here.

John: Ted, Henrietta, is the situation so urgent
that something must be done immediately?
How are your finances?

Ted: We can make it for awhile, but we'll have
to make some drastic changes if something

doesn't happen soon. I'm on jury duty next week so I couldn't go to Traverse till that's over or I'm excused.

John: I'll write George and send you all a copy. Also, Ted, you had better see Tom.

Ted: OK.

John: Ted, you won't be tied up on the jury all the time if it's like it usually is, so why don't you spend some time on the golf course with Bruce? Maybe you could all go down to Lois and Don's (daughter and son-in-law) this weekend. How're Jimmy and Sandy (grandchildren)?

Henrietta: Oh, they're fine, and Don is really studying and working.

John: Shall we leave it like this? You'll hear from me, and you'll see Tom. Your plans are set. OK.?

Ted: All right.

Henrietta: John, can we have prayer together?

John: Sure. (After prayer together, I left.)

Life has not been simple or easy for Ted and Henrietta recently. We discover that there is a high trust level between this couple and their former pastor, John Williams. It is probably because of this that he feels he can push so openly and directly in terms of "telling" them what to do. And it appears to have hit a responsive chord.

Questions for Discussion

John is quite active and directive in this encounter. Do you feel he is being too active in terms of becoming almost bossy? If this couple's conflict seems to be turned inward, what is his strategy in trying to relate them to Tom, George, Lois and Don, and so on? How sensitive is John to Ted and Henrietta? Do you feel John succeeded in enabling this couple to deal with their personal conflict? Why?

Sticks and Stones—Hurts and Love

Helen Rhoades is a young woman minister who spends some time each week working in an inner city community center with young children (six to nine years). The children are given opportunities for recreation, cultural enrichment, educational experiences, and so forth. One background factor which emerges in this encounter is that Billy has not paid his membership dues. (The dues are small, but the center staff feels they are symbolically important.) The setting is a late afternoon walk during the fall orientation program just after the schools have opened. Helen reports the following:

Helen: Come on, Nancy, let's go down here to get some leaves. (She trots down the road and three other children who have not paid their dues and are not part of the program follow her, but not Billy. Helen then feels something hitting her from the back and realizes that Billy is hitting her with small green berries from a tree. She ignores him at first, until he begins throwing them harder.) Billy, we don't throw things here. (He continues to throw them.) Billy, that hurts me and I don't like it; you stop. (Said quite calmly. Billy throws a few stones, then stops.)

Nancy: I want some of those pretty leaves up there.

Helen: I'll lift you up. (She does, and Nancy gets her leaf.)

Billy: I want to get a leaf too.

Helen: O.K., come here. (She lifts him up, and he gets a whole branch and pulls if off the tree. Then she set him down.)

Billy: (He hits Helen) You hurt me, you hurt my hand. (half angry, almost crying)

Helen: What? (Helen is taken aback, and just stands there looking at him for a few seconds. Billy sticks out his hand on which he has an open sore which is obviously infected.) Oh, I'm sorry. I didn't mean to hurt you.

Billy: Yes, you did. (very angry)

Nancy: No, I didn't. I'm really sorry. That looks like it's sore. I hope it will be all right. (pause) Why don't you play ball with some of the boys over there?

Billy: They won't let me.

Helen:	They won't let you?
Billy:	They said I can't because I haven't paid.
Helen:	No wonder you feel bad. Maybe you can pay soon; it's the beginning of the month. Do ask your mother. (he walks off)
Dorothy:	You haven't lifted me up to get a leaf.
Helen:	I think everybody got one.
Dorothy:	(Very angry) You didn't lift me. You didn't let me. You didn't lift me.
Helen:	(Looking at her carefully) You're right; up you go. (Helen lifts her)

A simple but touching example of what all of us sometimes do to win attention and, hopefully, favor. Obviously Billy is hurt (both physically and emotionally). He wants Helen to accept him but finds it difficult to come right out and say what he wants.

Questions for Discussion

As you read through this encounter, to what extent did you find yourself identifying with Helen and showing some impatience toward Billy? How do we begin to discover the difference between actions directed toward us, which are open anger and hostility, and those apparent disruptive behaviors which are intense efforts to gain our attention and acceptance? Can you recall the last time you employed this same technique to gain attention?

III   Accepting Faith Differences

The Christian church affirms considerable variety in faith stances. In discussing differences in our faith, generally we think of conflicts in doctrine or teaching about God, Jesus, the church, and so on. These differences are real, but they are not the only source of such controversy. There are at least three basic sources which yield faith differences. These are ideological, experiential, and interpretive.

Ideological differences show up at the formal confessional level. Discussion is couched in language about beliefs about Jesus, God, man, the church, whatever. Volumes of theological discourse, Sunday sermons, lay talks, and church school literature illustrate this source or mode of expression.

A second, and equally important, source of difference is experience. One may appeal to the validity and immediacy of his personal experience in lieu of, or over against, ideational or discursive sources. Differences arise out of the uniqueness of our individual experience. Indeed, the experience, feelings, and the intensity of perception create an emergent faith affirmation which has the quality of infallibility for the person. But this immediacy of experience carries the stamp of authenticity; it is a substantial source in faith affirmation.

A third source, interpretation, represents an obvious but important difference. Two or more people may interpret the same experience in strikingly contrasting ways.

We simply have to acknowledge that there may be two ways of looking at the same experience. A particular interpretation is but a puzzle piece from a larger picture, and ultimately this overall picture and perspective may be examined and perhaps challenged. But in a specific event sharp differences in interpretation may arise—and be entirely legitimate in that immediate situation as well as in the larger setting.

So the origins of faith differences arise not only out of what we formally believe and have carefully thought out in words. They also, and with equal validity, spring from our actual personal experience and/or how we interpret or make sense of our experience.

A word about our responses to differences in faith. Our response will move along a continuum from open antagonism to a positive change of attitude on our part, with a midpoint of dismissal. Here we simply give a shrug of the shoulder and forget about it. At the one end of our antagonism-conversion continuum is open hostility and anger. The polar opposite is open and warm acceptance. Midpoint is neutral, of course. Thus a response which moves toward either of the two extremes may be expressed in terms of a positive or negative reaction.

There are various ways in which we respond, as the following cases will illustrate. The important thing to remember at this point is that there will always be differences and conflict between what we and others believe. The multiplicity of sources for faith affirmation and the diversity of potential responses along the response continuum mean that there is a much greater pluralism in our common life as Christians than we generally realize. Thus, resolving conflict in faith differences is not so much a matter of elimination as of a carefully reasoned and a sensitively felt awareness that differences exist and have integrity.

Sight and Insight

The following case illustrates a conflict which frequently arises as people interpret the same experience differently. A young pastor, Alex Bury, shares the chaplain responsibilities in a community hospital and has come to know George Jones, who is a patient in Queenslace Hospital but not related to his church. Alex reports the following:

This individual is a thirty-year-old Caucasian who has entered the hospital as a referral patient. He was very congenial but had a definite speech problem. He had to struggle physically to manage the simplest short phrases. He was also partially blind, being able to see only vague images. I was informed that he had had a pressure growth on the medulla oblongata which was responsible for his speech and sight difficulties. He was scheduled to undergo surgery in a couple of days. He was married and the father of two children: a daughter, eleven and a son, five.

As I approached the patient, I noticed that he was sitting on the edge of the bed. He had not been able to do so before. As I approached, he smiled, but little did I realize what was to follow.

George: Hi again, Chaplain.

Alex: Hi, Mr. Jones. How are you feeling today? (Being in my usual abstract state of mind, the astonishment at the patient being able to recognize me and talk had not yet struck.)

George: Better than when you were here yesterday.

Alex: My! Your speech problem has improved. What have they done for you? (surprised at last)

George: Yeah, I can talk a lot better, and I can see you too. They say my sight will keep getting better all along. Down at the eye clinic they said I probably would not even have to wear glasses.

Alex: That is great! You can talk so much easier today. You could hardly say a word yesterday.

George: Yeah, it's great! It sure is great to be like this again. It has sure been a long time since I could talk and see this well.

Alex: It must be great. There sure has been a big change—what happened?

George: I guess I just have to give the Lord credit. They took me down to x-ray to give me some treatment. They were going to operate tomorrow. But they won't have to now. They say I am going to keep improving and that my eyesight will probably even be 20-20.

Alex: When did you realize that you could see and talk?

George: When they brought me back from x-ray and I woke up. I could see soon after that, but things were blurry. I can see real good now; those cards on the wall, I can read them real clear.

Alex: Did they expect the x-ray treatment to help you be able to see and talk this well?

George: No, they were just doing some work before the operation. They say I should keep improving. It sure is great! Those doctors were as surprised as I was; I always heard that if you have enough faith, everything will turn out all right. I know it is true *now*. (emphasis) I can't thank God enough for healing me.

Alex: The feeling of faith is easier to have since you are improving, I suppose?

George: Yes, it is. I have been bothered with this since I was about fifteen, and I just kept getting worse until I became like I was yesterday. They said my only hope was to have that operation. I am glad I won't have to now. It feels so great. God sure did work a miracle for me. I always believed he could do it, but now I know because he healed me.

Alex: You place a lot of faith in God now, but I suppose it was pretty difficult before.

George: Yes, it was—but I have no doubt now. God did what those doctors could not do. I can't thank him enough! I have never really been able to see my five-year-old boy. Now I can see and talk to him. It is going to be a big change. I am so thankful that God healed me.

Alex: Had the doctors not helped your condition before you came into the hospital this time?

George: Not really. I just kept getting worse—but things are going to be different now.

Alex: Since God stepped in, everything has changed, I suppose. I guess it did not seem like he was there before, uh?

George: It was hard to have faith then, but it won't be anymore. Only God could do this for me. I just can't wait to get back home.

Alex: Even having faith in God will be easier now. I guess you feel like a walking example of what God can do. Along with your new faith in God it will probably be easier to have faith about other things in life.

George: It sure is great. No one can imagine how it feels. God did what no one else could do for me.

Alex: You feel like God took over in the doctor's place. I guess that is what resulted in your miraculous recovery, uh?

George: I sure do. It was simply a miracle! I have heard about miracles, but now I have experienced it. It's so great!

For all practical purposes, the conversation continued along this line until we terminated the visit. The next visit with this patient could have easily been recorded as a ditto mark of this one in that the responses and jubilant attitude of Mr. Jones continued.

Alex comments as follows on this conversation:

In looking at this encounter one must take into consideration the abrupt and tremendous change in the patient's condition. Understandably, the element of surprise dominated this encounter. I was caught off guard, not at all expecting to be confronted with this type of recovery instead of illness. The patient was almost in a frantic state of hysteria over his truly miraculous recovery and was projecting all his thoughts upon the future. As the visit progressed I felt that he had not "come down" long enough to realize the happenings of the moment or to speculate rationally about the future. In view of the circumstances, I feel this was to be expected. After a debilitating illness he was anticipating a promising future.

Alex demonstrates his concern for George and shows some insight into the dynamics of this encounter and certainly of his own feelings; one gets the impression that he remains too clinical and detached. Alex has insight, while George Jones has discovered both new sight and a new vision. Somehow, the two men seem never really to get together in this encounter.

Questions for Discussion

How do you feel about the way Alex, as pastor and chaplain, responds to Mr. Jones? To what extent do you sense a tug-of-war between their respective views of "the miraculous" in the Christian life? How would you respond in this situation? (as George? as Alex?) Why?

Whose Problem Is It?

John Smith is the minister with youth at Grace Church, which is located in a college town. John speaks candidly of a situation in which he can appreciate both sides of some rather basic faith differences between him and Sean Dixon, a university student. He would like to dismiss the problem but can't; he feels somewhat antagonistic but knows he shouldn't. He wants some change in attitude on his part but is afraid of how that might shake his own faith. John puts it this way.

The dynamics of this situation are related to a most unusual person; they include him, members of my youth group, and me.

Sean is the son of Indian parents; he was converted to Christianity from Hinduism. At the college this past year he was an experimental subject with the parapsychology department. He is a psychic whose power includes reading persons' past and future, ESP, and, supposedly, faith healing. Sean sees these powers as gifts from God and is not out to exploit people. He joined Grace Church and became a close friend of the minister to youth. The extent of his contact with youth varied greatly. He has a childlike faith (simple, literal, unquestioning) based upon his own unique insights. I have reacted as a skeptic; a few of the young people who last spring experienced an emotion-laden conversion seem to be caught up in Sean's visionary spiritualism.

The problem is complex. Basically it concerns the interaction between Sean and me, Sean and the group, the group and me. I do not want to cut Sean off from the fellowship of the church, nor do I want to alienate him from me. But I see possible bad effects on the youth, and I cannot, as a theologian and minister, go along with certain of the priorities Sean insists upon. I am perplexed about how to help foster growth beyond adolescent religious experience, and how, as a theologian and friend, to fit myself into that search. Also, I can't help wondering, "What if Sean is right?"

BRIEF ANALYSIS

A. Sean: How to preserve his link with the church and deal realistically with his powers. Many in the church are close to him. Should I try to cultivate his friendship? What about faith healing and Sean's desire to have a prayer group expressly for that purpose?

B. Youth: How to foster growth when they are wrapped up in phrases like "know Christ," "accept him," and "I can't describe the feeling." How to provide for their need (which I recognize and want to meet) for fellowship, sharing, and Bible study. How to handle inter-group friction and hostility from those who are turned off by this evangelical emphasis.

C. Me: A need for a more disciplined spiritual life and feeling that a minister should do more than referee personality clashes (i.e., that our problem may be one of disbelief). How do all aspects relate to my various roles?

Certainly the word "complex" describes this problem. It is obvious that John has given considerable and careful thought to this problem and is not anxious to move too quickly to resolve it, lest a greater problem arise. But still a basic conflict is there.

Questions for Discussion

John seems to have boxed the compass in terms of trying to consider as much as possible in his analysis. Now, where would you go in terms of resolving the problem? What would be the anticipated consequences? And what would you do about them?

The Gates of Hell Shall Not Prevail

A minister often finds it difficult to pastor one flock or one congregation where he may assume some common ground among members' beliefs and their social and personal lives. But take the following situation. The Reverend David Camp has been employed by a group of churches to serve as weekend minister at a campground. We all know that the leisure weekend away from the home church is very much on the increase. At home we miss people who have gone on the weekend, whether it may be to camp, to ski, to snowmobile, or whatever. Faith differences within a local church can become rather intense at times, as we know. Dave tells us what it's like in a campground ministry.

His situation is fairly typical. Camp Honeybee is located some twenty-five miles outside a major metropolitan area. It is a fairly well developed and stable camp. That is, there are a number of trailers kept permanently at the camp, with the owners commuting from the city on weekends. Some people, whose work schedule permits, will spend Friday through Monday at the camp. For these people, this is an inexpensive summer place and becomes almost a second home. For the others Honeybee is simply a stopping place for one or several nights for the family on a vacation trip. Thus Dave meets people of different theological and socio-economic levels and with varying degrees of understanding in his parish.

There are five people with whom Dave has spent considerable time, and who typify the diversity of faith differences in this parish.

Kenneth Waddle is a middle-aged businessman, a devoted layman who took the initiative to address Dave —as soon as he discovered he was the campground pastor—with the question, "Do you believe in the Virgin Birth?" Nothing else; just that. And every weekend a discussion about the Virgin Birth must precede any other conversation. Then out tumbles an endless cascade of religious talk.

Edgar O'Brien is an intense young white-collar worker who is convinced of the powers of ESP and psychosomatic medicine for religious purposes. In his sharing group back home he claims hypnotic states are achieved so that diagnosis and healing of diseases can occur. Certainly Dave could gain no better training in religious skills than what Edgar has, and so each weekend he tries to convert and recruit Mr. Camp for "the group."

Wanda Spiritos is unwavering in her belief that all souls were created at one time and inhabit several bodies. Her intense conviction and charm greet Dave weekly.

Ted McLean is a retired disabled truck driver and never had much contact with or use for the church before establishing his quasi-permanent residence at Honeybee and his contact with Dave. He has a warm and groping and awkward faith. He depends heavily on Dave for growth in his newfound belief.

Tommy Clippinger is a young adolescent who comes from the city on weekends with his family. He continually admonishes Dave to preach on how to get to heaven and is not bashful in expressing his disappointment when such sermons are not forthcoming.

This is Dave's problem—such diversity and such unity. There is no way one pastor's faith could honestly embrace these different beliefs, and yet the minister has to, somehow. His is a ministry to a nonsectarian campground. He must speak with conviction, but he cannot castigate those whose beliefs are deep and strong and fundamentally different from his own and others at Honeybee.

What amazes, perplexes, and disturbs is why these people, who hold such obvious differences in beliefs, all faithfully attend the campground worship services.

Questions for Discussion

It seems quite clear from these five very brief belief sketches that there are radical faith differences in the camp. Why is it that all come together to worship? Can they do so in good conscience? What is it they really see in Dave Camp, this detached weekend pastor? Are they letting their hair down? Do they see Dave as a theological pushover? How do you feel about people like Dave Camp or Wanda or Edgar when you're away from home? What does this say about our faith differences?

IV   Recognizing Church Staff Conflicts

An area of potential controversy in the local church is the staff. Any group of persons working together are certain from time to time to experience some degree of tension and conflict. Personality clashes may occur between individual members. The personal goals of a member of the staff may conflict with those of the group. The staff may have somewhat different goals than those of the larger organization for which they are working. A senior member of the staff may be arbitrary and domineering, causing resentment and controversy among his subordinates.

There are several reasons why a church staff may be particularly susceptible to conflict. One is the perception which persons who enter religious professions, particularly the ministry, have of their task. The individual may select this profession with a profound sense of dedication. He may feel that he has been called of God to preach the gospel. Because the individual is in a relatively low paying occupation, rewards come in the form of what he can accomplish in the church. Thus, the combination of strong feelings about his "calling" and the fact that payment comes mainly in the realization of goals rather than financial remuneration makes the church staff an area of potential conflict.

Related to this is the kind of image that men entering the ministry have of their role, an image which is also reinforced by many aspects of theological education. The clergyman may see himself as the pastor in charge. The successful minister is something of a performer. Every Sunday he conducts a service and is the center of attention as he delivers the sermon for that day. Furthermore, he occupies a central role in his community. He is asked to be present and participate in a range of civic functions. He is called upon for advice and counsel from many persons on a variety of problems. Even the most humble minister cannot but be aware that he is perceived to be a person of some importance. When several persons with such experience are placed in a church staff and expected to work closely together, each to some degree being subordinate to the other, conflict may occur.

Another factor contributing to potential conflict among members of a church staff is the kind of brotherly democratic ideology which many religious professionals hold. The operation of a staff requires some line of authority. Members of the staff may be reluctant to deal with the recalcitrant individual because such action would seem inconsistent with their concept of brotherliness. A senior member may hestitate to exercise his authority because it might appear undemocratic. The result sometimes is to postpone dealing with the real issues, which over the long term may reduce the total effectiveness of the staff and hurt individual members as well.

Successful participation in a church staff requires the individuals to accept the fact that they are surrendering a degree of autonomy for the greater goals of the group. It requires the realization that no group can be conflict free, even a church staff motivated by the gospel. It necessitates the realistic acceptance of conflict as a phenomenon which must be understood and handled in a manner which will contribute to the goals of the group.

A Call to Arms or a Call to Worship

Here we have Harmony Church with a small but active congregation. The Reverend John Henry comes to Harmony as pastor, and the following events begin to unfold. First of all, when he begins to prepare for his first Sunday worship service, he discovers that the previous minister, along with Mrs. Marvel, the choir director and organist, have prepared bulletins for the following three weeks. Second, he discovers the actual authority of the choir director. The previous pastor had granted her complete freedom to choose all hymns and music and to prepare the order of service itself. This included the use of another denomination's Communion ritual because the director was the member of that fellowship. None of these arrangements had been questioned by nor were they common knowledge among the congregation.

Mr. Henry reports the following developments which led to a painful showdown after more than a year at the Harmony parish.

During the First Year—I picked out hymns but always asked the choir director if they were known to the congregation. Most of the time when I requested a new hymn, I was told the congregation could not sing it. I would then ask the choir to learn it and teach it to the congregation. But this rarely happened. One night at choir practice a member of the choir said she thought this was unfair to me, and an effort was made by the choir director to teach a new hymn. Some in choir would complain they couldn't sing the new hymn, so plans were dropped.

Complication—The organ and piano were both played during morning worship, but the piano dominated and often would drown out the organ and congregational singing. The piano was played by the choir director. The choir director had been requested by me to learn the musical setting of the United Methodist Communion service. This was not done, and I spoke to the choir and the choir director, and she said she thought that was a lot of "hog wash." Most of the musical settings sung by the choir were by John Peterson or were gospel hymn tunes.

The choir director/organist resigned for the summer and was replaced by a couple who had recently joined the church. Mrs. Marvel, the previous director, then asked for her job back to start a youth choir on her own. She bought uniforms for youth choir members and was going to take them out witnessing.

I objected to her charging parents for dress material. Further, Mrs. Marvel submitted a bill to the church for sixty dollars worth of music materials after she was no longer director.

In this case we are concerned about two things. First are the dynamics of a staff conflict; a second concern is that the whole worship and music program of the congregation became the arena for a staff struggle. Not only were innocent people involved, but the implications of the original conflict had a snowballing effect so that after a year everyone was caught up in the fight, all becoming angry, confused, and frustrated. But no one knew where to apply a tourniquet of reasonable and controlled discussion in order to prevent, if not to slow down, this rupture in the lifeblood of the local congregation. Finally, Mr. Henry simply politically overpowered the former director as senior staff person in order to establish order and to bring life and hope back to Harmony. If this approach had been used earlier, the long and involved struggle may have been prevented.

Several possible avenues could have been explored earlier. (1) Every church has, or should have, a music or worship committee. Mr. Henry could have asked this group to convene to hear out the conflict and he could have asked for its counsel. It could be that the committee would have supported him, or it might have gone along with the director, Mrs. Marvel. Thus Mr. Henry would have known earlier the sentiments and beliefs of this representative group. (2) Most churches have some form of a pastor-parish relations committee. Here, this group also could have been used in an advisory capacity. It could have provided wise counsel about the feelings and beliefs of the congregation and reflected on its goals for the church. (3) The pastor might have called a congregational meeting or asked to have the governing body of the church deal with this conflict earlier in his tenure simply to force the issue into the open. But having pursued none of these alternatives in dealing with the conflict between himself and Mrs. Marvel, Mr. Henry kept the problem on an interpersonal level.

Questions for Discussion

As a stranger in a new congregation, what could Mr. Henry have done, after discovering this conflict with Mrs. Marvel, to deal with it immediately? If you were a new minister with strong, positive views about worship, music, and liturgy and the administrative body of your church voted to support the director and not you, how would you feel and what would you do about this defeat? Would it be fair in this case to say that time does not heal everything and is ultimately on the side of those who deal with conflict, not of those who try to avoid it?

Who's in Charge Here?

Ben Jones was on the staff of the Church of the Redeemer. His responsibilities had been carefully detailed and understood by him and his supervisor, the Reverend Thomas Timothy. One of Mr. Jones's tasks was to conduct a Sunday evening seminar discussion group on the meaning of death for the Christian. From the beginning it was clear on paper that Jones would be in charge, both as resource person (providing the content materials) and as discussion leader.

But Jones reports that as the seminar developed, Pastor Timothy continued to interrupt discussion, altering the direction of thought. Generally these disruptions were detrimental to the group. They tended to patronize Jones, his material, and the group members. The general thrust or theme of Timothy's comments would be "what is Christian about this," then inserting something like, "the Christian would believe . . ." Finally Ben decided he needed to confront Mr. Timothy directly, in private conversation, about these interruptions and interjections and their negative effect both on himself and on the group's ability to consider the issues being presented.

Ben made an appointment to see his supervisor, and this conversation occurs at the Timothy residence.

Ben: I know we disagree strongly about what I've been doing in the seminar. I'm sure you think I'm not talking about the Christian understanding of death. (he nods yes) Nevertheless, I have an agenda I need to deal with—some things I think are important. I'd like a chance to talk about our differences after the sessions . . .

Tom: (interrupting) Yes, I know. Even though I disagree, your contract says it's your seminar—so you can do it how you want to. I know I get on my soapbox from time to time. Would you like to know why I've been doing that?

Ben: Yes.

Tom: After the first one, some of the older people were pretty upset. Mrs. Able, Mrs. Baker, and Miss Campbell all talked to me about it. All I was trying to do was to put some kind of positive note in for them. Perhaps your approach is O.K. for the younger people, but for older people, I think you ought not try to do this. I suppose I was just being too protective. I know you think I'm threatened by all this talk about death, but I'm not. I used to be pretty easy to shock, but not anymore. Since I've been in the ministry, I've been so mixed up with death that I'm not shocked or threatened by it. I know I have some trouble visiting people with cancer who are dying. It's all I can do to go to the hospital. (He talked almost ten minutes more relating his experiences and expressing his feelings about death and ministering to dying persons.) Let's plan on meeting after this in order to talk about it some more.

In reflecting upon this encounter, Ben Jones reported,

I went to his house to free myself from a bad situation and ended up freeing a flood of his feelings about death and dying persons. His words almost tumbled out, and any comments I had prepared were never made—there was no need or place for them. The problem for him, I think, was that he had begun to doubt his own statements about joyously accepting death with no need to grieve if we are Christian, etc. This seminar had served to facilitate his thinking and bring to the surface many problems he has had.

By putting his foot down, Ben Jones confronted his supervisor, Tom Timothy, with how little trust was being placed in him to lead the seminar. This "show down" allowed Ben to maintain his integrity as the seminar leader. It had the secondary and positive effect of enabling Tom to come to terms with his defensive theology of death and dying and to discover the ways he was protecting himself while bludgeoning others to joyous submission. If Ben Jones, the junior staff person, had avoided this difficult conflict, the resolution would have been destructive for everyone: the seminar and group discussion would always be blocked; Tom would have been stuck with playing the role of the all-knowing pastor and been prevented from entering into serious conversation about death and dying, including his own fears about ministry to the dying.

The resolution in this case yielded several very positive results: Ben did not have to worry about distracting interruptions; Thomas had a fellow pastor in whom he could begin to confide and with whom he could share his theology of death; and the laymen of the church could deal with the theological issues about death instead of being bystanders to a battle between Ben and Thomas.

Questions for Discussion

We often talk about our willingness to allow the younger people, whether on a staff or in a family or in a job, to develop their own beliefs and style of doing things. But how often do we find ourselves in Pastor Timothy's position? When we are in Ben's situation, do we simply submit and chafe at the bit? If not, does Ben's approach seem plausible? Why or why not?

The Soft Sell Is Not Soft Soap

Bill Willing had been interviewed for a staff position, and his general impressions of the senior pastor, Ronald

Regular, were favorable. Apparently Mr. Regular expressed low-key expectations in the job. That is, the programs were generally established and smooth running. There were no immediate difficulties, and Bill could expect to step in and assume previously defined and accepted leadership roles in the major areas of his responsibilities. The senior man had not indicated during the interview that there were any significant unresolved issues which would trouble or plague the new man. Well, what more can one ask? So Mr. Willing accepted the new position with high hopes.

On the surface all seemed much in accord with the reports and expectations as Mr. Regular described them. Nothing abrasive occurred; but before long, Bill began to detect that Ronald really expected much more than he stated. Oh, the programs were congruent with the interview discussions, but the focus of leadership style expectations became troublesome. It seems as though Mr. Regular, instead of being the low-key nice guy, had very specific and exacting ways in which the staff should conduct and assert itself in its pastoral and leadership roles. The issue boiled down to this: Bill is to do all the leading, especially in youth work and various discussion groups, whether with youth or other groups.

Bill had assumed that one of his responsibilities was to cultivate lay leadership and expression and had set about to accomplish this. But no. Mr. Regular insisted that the pastors give very direct and immediate guidance to all phases of the church's programs and group life. Of course this was contrary to Bill's theology of the church, especially that of the laity and how he saw himself as a minister of the gospel.

Here we have a very strong but in many ways subtle conflict. Ronald Regular appears to run a low-key operation and staff relations. But that kind of cool touch belies the intensity of conviction and pressure behind the scenes to remain always low-key, regardless of the kinds of problems and differences that may arise. So Mr. Regular is a nice guy, to be sure; but surely his pleasant, easy-going manner communicates in subtle but substantive ways that he is a nice guy so long as you agree with him and do things his way.

It's very difficult to pick up this kind of multilevel operation in a single interview or encounter because Ronald is so polished at keeping the rough edges and demanding pressures veiled with his convincing genteel manner—a style of relating which tends to captivate us all. Bill's choice falls along the lines of one of two alternatives. Either he can call Ronald's bluff, or he can call a spade a spade.

This would mean, on the one hand, that Bill would confront Ronald with his impression that under the smooth veneer of his nice programs, Ronald is scared to death to let anyone do anything that might reveal that the church, or the pastor, or the members are not in perfect order—cool, calm, and collected. Here the bluff dimension would be that the pastor is creating his own golden calf, made in his image or the one he would like to have of himself, for the people to worship. This distracts him and the congregation from confronting such basic issues as "difference," "failure," "priesthood of all believers," and so forth.

On the calling a spade a spade dimension, Bill could confront Regular with the integrity of his own ministry and theology, so that in good conscience he would have to develop lay leadership and acknowledge differences and failures in the church's life. There's more than a little Martin Luther in this kind of stand, but it constitutes the other basic way Bill Willing has of resolving this serious problem, both theologically and interpersonally. Here, the difference between them would simply have to ride.

Questions for Discussion

Do people generally consider you or pastors you know nice guys? Does the case of Bill Willing and Ronald Regular shed any light on the kind of interests being protected and exploited in the "nice guy" situations you've been in? Do you see any authoritarianism here? Have you ever found yourself in the leadership position of being the nice-guy-so-long-as-you-agree-with-me type of person? And have you ever thought how this reflects on the priesthood-of-all-believers motif?

Promotion as a Preoccupation

Sam Strong had joined the staff of a large parish as an associate and was initially impressed by the quality of the church life. He immersed himself deeply in the programs and was especially conscientious in his staff responsibilities. All went well for a considerable time. But eventually Sam reports that while he thought he was doing his work well, he began having trouble trying to determine how well he was actually doing in the eyes of his boss. Sam relates the following about Dr. George Gunner, the boss:

He is young, dynamic, domineering, and somewhat authoritarian, extremely competent, and a candidate for bishop someday (my guess is that he has a similar perspective). To date, our relationship has been stormy. At times I feel like I'm doing all right, yet most of the time I feel like I'm under his judgment and am not measuring up. I have confronted him with this. He said he didn't know how I was doing, yet he had vibrations that the quality of relationship with the teachers was not good. He did not have a source for this. Other criticisms would include: (1) lack of careful editing and word usage in letters to congregation; (2) a too personal style in sermons and in letters to the congregation he doesn't like being folksy.

In a way, I am deeply suspicious of what's going on since I am being evaluated for continuation next year. I will be setting up a peer group seminar to check out where I am in relation to the congregation. This I look forward to, but what bothers me is that I am very much under his shadow. I attend meetings, attend worship, and so forth, but do not lead in them. Dr. Gunner promises more participation as time goes on (an empty promise I heard my second year at seminary in a different place). I feel the possibility of losing my confidence in relating to people on my own basis as a personal, caring human being. (This is my number one priority.) He comes on as strong, somewhat aloof, doing all the right things, and saying the right things as rector. This threatens—I need to feel important and needed and need to assert my own style of ministry. The universal issue for me then is:

When confronted with a strong and competent superior, I tend to let him tell me what to do, even though I don't like what he says, because I'm afraid of losing the debate (accepting is not losing). This is demeaning to me, and I recognize it, but I fear the consequences of my actions if I should confront him. (1) Looking like a fool (his positions are always thought-out). (2) Feeling more inferior than I already feel. (3) Coming to terms with the possibility that maybe I don't fit in or am not competent or acceptable enough for the demands of the situation.

This is where I am. As you can see, I am confused and bitter. The hostility I have is not productive, and it scares me. In a way, I fear that either I have to be my own boss (no judgment or evaluation of my work) or have a loose, fluid peer relationship, not that of superior to subordinate, to function effectively.

This particular problem was shared with a group of Sam's ministerial peers. Contrary to some of Sam's feelings toward himself—he was afraid he would lose a debate, look like a fool, feel inferior, and so on—the peer group saw the relation and tension between Dr. Gunner and Sam Strong as a conflict over Sam's strength and competence, not over his leadership inadequacies and dependency needs. Strangely enough, Sam seemed to possess many of the characteristics ascribed to and discovered in Dr. Gunner, who was a good ministerial leader. The source of conflict and friction, as the group saw it, was that Sam was doing a very good job but that Dr. Gunner wanted to claim credit and reap the ecclesiastical harvest in terms of his own preoccupation with promotion, perhaps ultimately the episcopacy.

The situation that emerged was that Sam was very effective and—ironically, because of his competence— was threatening the "gung-ho" leadership of Gunner: someone else could perform pastoral responsibilities as well as the rector. So it was not Sam who was weak, but Gunner with his political and ecclesiastical aspirations who was threatened.

Father Gunner may have had his eyes on the episcopacy. But others of us may likewise have our eyes on significant promotions or changes so that we become supersensitive to excellent work by our subordinates, not wanting them to enjoy the credit that is theirs, but instead trying to deflect that excellence onto our own broad and ambitious shoulders.

These conflicts and interpersonal transactions crop up in the full-time multiple-staff church administrations; similarly, the same conflicts may be at work among various leaders within any parish. Or perhaps occupational, political, social, and civic rivalries which have their rootage in a secular setting are brought into the church and some very significant lay or secular battles are fought within the church setting. Technically this may not be church business, but the conflict occurs openly in a church and pastoral setting. So we bring our preoccupations and aspirations, whether ecclesiastical, political, personal, to the church, and we need to be aware that the Dr. Gunner and Sam Strong kind of battles and feelings frequently occur.

Questions for Discussion

Do you know of similar situations to the Gunner-Strong conflict? What happened, and how, in the light of the above, could this conflict be resolved? To what extent do you act like George Gunner when in his position, and how does it feel to be an unappreciated Sam Strong? Sam cracked open this problem by bringing his conflict to a peer group; would a peer group be helpful for your church?

V   Untangling Pastor-Parish Relations

The relationship of the pastor to the members of his parish is an area of continuing tension within the local church. There are many reasons for this. One is the number of persons within the parish to whom the pastor and his wife must relate. Among the two hundred to two thousand individuals there are certain to be a portion who do not get along with any particular clergyman. In virtually every congregation are a few persons who love the previous pastor and resent the present one.

More important as a source of pastor-parish conflict are the differing views held by pastor and people of what the church is and what it should be doing. The minister will have specific ideas about the nature of the church and its role in society. He has thought much about this; probably he had a course in this subject in theological seminary. He wants his congregation to be moving in the direction that he believes to be the wave of the future. He may perceive his church members as troops whom he will lead in the struggle for desirable social change.

The lay persons may have a completely different concept of what the church is all about. Certainly they will not have reached their understanding of the church by reading the latest books on the subject. They are more likely to have secured this information from their days in the Sunday school and their experience in a particular congregation. The laymen may see the church as a source of stability in a society characterized by rapid social change. It would be possible for a pastor to see the church as an instrument of social change and his laymen to view it as a protector of the status quo. In point of fact, the cases of a pastor and his people having completely different views of the church are infrequent. A congregation tends not to call, or a bishop tends not to appoint, a minister whose views would obviously so clash with those of the laymen that the subsequent conflict would impair the ministry of that church. Nevertheless, degrees of difference in their understanding of the nature, purpose, and goals of the church are frequent sources of pastor-parish conflict.

Every congregation is made up not only of individuals but also of groups. The individual has a membership not only in the congregation as a whole but in several groups within the total church. Thus a person not only joins the Grace Baptist Church, he may also become a part of the Fellowship Sunday School Class, the men's club, the finance committee, and the choir. Participation in most of the activities in any local church is through one of the groups organized around age (the youth fellowship), sex (the men's club), special interest (the choir), or specific task (the committee on education). With the exception of the worship service which all members are expected to attend, the individual's church participation tends to be through groups within the larger congregation.

That some groups do from time to time develop rivalries and get into conflicts with other groups should be no surprise. The very nature of congregational organization brings persons of similar characteristics and interests together. This tends to maximize the differences between the groups. Age differences may be manifest in the attempt of the older board members to restrict the activities of the youth fellowship. The more liberal or conservative individual tends to gravitate to the study group he finds most congenial. The gathering of like-minded persons can exaggerate the differences between groups with a different outlook on life. And in virtually every group conflict the pastor is involved either as participant or victim.

This chapter will deal with conflict involving the pastor and individuals and groups within the congregation. Included will be cases involving a different interpretation of what the pastor should be doing, the continued return of a beloved former pastor, and the opposition of a group in the church to a program started by the pastor.

Prophet vs. Profits

The pastor-parish relations committee was meeting to decide whether or not to request that their pastor be reappointed for another year. The minister was not present. The chairman opened the session: "You know the purpose of this meeting. We need to decide what recommendation concerning the appointment of Bill Abbott we want to make to the bishop. If we want him back next year, we should ask that he be reappointed. If we want a different minister, we can request one. What are your opinions on this matter?"

There was a long period of silence. This was broken by Ed Wilcox, the chairman of the finance committee: "I expect we might as well face the fact that our church is not doing well. When Bill Abbott came to St. Andrew's three years ago, we had 569 members; now our membership is 525. We have had a continual problem with finances. Our income has not kept up with inflation. There are only two months left in this fiscal year, and we are about 30 percent behind in income to meet our budget."

Mrs. Sarah Evans, the president of the women's organization, was unhappy with what she felt was an attack on the minister. "I don't think we can blame Mr. Abbott for our financial problems. Our people like him and appreciate what he has done. We all know there has been a nationwide decline in church participation. We aren't any different."

The discussion continued for some time with some persons voicing criticism of the pastor and others expressing appreciation for his services and pointing out his strengths. It was apparent that the pastor had a small group of most ardent supporters. Even these persons showed by their comments that they were aware that all was not well within the congregation. The membership was decreasing, participation in worship and other activities had dropped, and it was evident that the budget would not be met.

Tom Ward, the chairman of the social concerns committee and a strong supporter of the pastor, had said very little during the meeting up to this point. "We haven't talked about the real issue. Every one of us knows what the problem is, but nobody has said it. The reason why some people have stopped coming is Bill Abbott's stand against the war. Some of those who disagree with him have dropped out. We have got to decide if we are going to stand by our pastor or sacrifice him to appease the people who want a military victory."

Mary Dexter, who headed the evangelism committee, offered a contrary opinion: "I think this situation is more complex than you make it sound. I happen to share Bill Abbott's opinions about the war. I think I also understand something of the depth of his feelings. But I also have to admit that he has put a great deal of time into these activities."

Ed Wilcox, one of the more outspoken critics of the pastor, responded: "You know that Mr. Abbott and I do not see eye to eye on the war. We knew his position before he came here. I was a member of this committee when we interviewed him. And I voted that we request his appointment. As I see it, he is spending too much time on the war issue and neglecting other things, especially since he became chairman of the Committee of Antiwar Christians last year."

Mary Dexter then continued: "As chairman of the evangelism committee, I must admit that Bill Abbott has not followed up on prospective members as I would have liked. His participation in the antiwar movement has been a major interest and has taken a great deal of his time. Some other things simply have not gotten attention."

Tom Ward, with a great deal of emotion, responded: "But we cannot tell our minister that he should give up his antiwar activities. I know how he feels about this. If it means that people won't come to church, let them stay home. We are better off without them. The church has got to stand for something, even if it loses support. What is the church all about anyway? I am not going to sit quiet and let this committee persecute our minister."

The chairman of the committee intervened: "It is getting late, and I think we ought to bring this discussion to a close soon. Let me summarize where we seem to be as a committee. There is a concern about the membership and financial trends. We are all a bit uneasy about what is happening, or rather what is not happening. Some of you feel that our pastor is spending too much time on one aspect of his ministry, the antiwar movement, and neglecting some others. I can honestly say that I don't feel that any of us object to his stand on the war, even those who have a different view. I don't think we are ready to make a recommendation on his appointment for next year. I would suggest that we call another meeting as soon as possible with Bill here so we can discuss the matter with him."

Questions for Discussion

Is the drop in membership, attendance, and giving the result of the pastor's antiwar stand or his failure to give attention to other aspects of ministry? Is the proposal that the committee discuss this matter with the pastor desirable? If you were the pastor, how do you think you would react? Is there a danger that this issue might be the source of a serious conflict in the congregation? How might this situation be handled in a constructive manner?

The Return of the False Messiah

A rather angry young pastor, Charles Sterling, refers to a former minister as a "false messiah." He describes for a group of ministers with whom he meets regularly the details surrounding his feelings.

Though the term "false messiah" overstates the case, it is somewhat descriptive. Certain people in my church feel a strong attachment to a former minister of twelve years ago. I have been pastor of this church since last June. I have had five funerals, and he has been back for three. Two of these I had no idea that he had been invited to conduct.

This is not the major problem, however. I can put up with the guy for an hour at a funeral. But to associate with him and be an accessory to a week of nightly services conducted by this man is simply more than I could allow. He is a very nice man, but he is simply not what this church needs as a revival speaker. I feel I must be able to work freely with the visiting speaker and would not be able to do so with this man. A revival is not a homecoming, and his return at this time would simply be a week-long homecoming. I am not jealous of the man and ordinarily would not mind his being here. However, if I am going to support a revival, I must feel it has every chance of being real and meaningful from the start.

The church, or rather a group within the congregation, would definitely prefer that he be the speaker. This has been made plain to me. I am confident that it was generally accepted that he would be coming for the revival. I stated Sunday night at the board meeting that I had invited someone else, and upon request gave my reasons. Opposition was minimal. Except for facial expressions and two verbal responses, there was really none.

My concern is that although little opposition to my decision was expressed, the revival will not be supported. Even if no one should come during the entire week, I would do the same thing next year regarding this man.

I must add that I am and have been from the start very well accepted by the people. Both the attendance and the offerings are up considerably from past years. Generally the people are behind me in my ministry. I say this simply to support the fact that I am not jealous of this or any other former pastor.

Questions for Discussion

While we may feel that Charles Sterling is overreacting to the former pastor, can we not all identify with the problem? The focal point may not have been a revival speaker, but there are the funerals, weddings, holiday social visits, well-timed impromptu appearances at group meetings, and so on which kick up some of the feelings which Charles is describing. But what to do about it—that is the question.

Perhaps we can easily identify with the feelings of

resentment and frustration associated with calling someone a false messiah. But at times former pastors have
been a source of extreme comfort and benefit both to
the current pastor and to the congregation. What makes
the difference between seeing the return of a former pastor as that of a false messiah or a divine comforter? Do
the laymen of a church have a responsibility to be sensitive to the new pastor so that the false-messiah motif may
be approached constructively for everyone? How is this
done?

But Not in This Church

Shady Grove is a small Methodist church located in
a predominantly rural community. With a membership of
sixty-one, it is the smallest of the three congregations
served by the same minister. The majority of the members are old; many are retired farmers and widows of
farmers. The church has little program other than the
Sunday worship service. The Sunday school was discontinued five years ago because there were not enough
children to warrant keeping it in operation.

When a new pastor was appointed to serve the three
churches, he took a careful look at the community. He
discovered that there were three different groups of people living in the area served by Shady Grove Church.
First were the persons who made up the majority of the
members. Second, there were a number of white families
where the father, and sometimes the mother, worked in

a large textile mill located in a nearby town. These families tended to be younger than the majority of the church members, and they had a number of children who could attend a Sunday school if one were available. Some members of the mill families did attend church, but only one held any official position—membership on the pastor-parish relations committee.

The third group in the community were Indians. No church was currently ministering to these persons. There were a large number of Indian children about whom the pastor felt the church should be concerned.

The pastor decided that the best way to begin serving the mill worker and Indian families was to organize a program for the children. From a nearby college he recruited several students to serve as teachers. He then told the Shady Grove people that he was planning to have a community-wide Sunday school type program but that it would be held on Saturday afternoon. There were no objections to this proposal.

With two Volkswagen Microbuses, one owned by the pastor and the other by one of the students, a group of children were picked up and brought to Shady Grove Church for a Saturday afternoon program. Within a few weeks approximately eighty children were attending the Saturday afternoon "Sunday school." Three fourths of those coming were Indian; the children whose parents worked in the mill made up the remaining participants.

Everything went well for almost four months. Then one Friday the local high school had a racial incident involving white and black students. In an effort to reduce tensions, all the town pastors were requested to come to the high school to serve as mediators. It also happened to be the day of Shady Grove Church's annual barbecue. As the group of members worked during the day in preparation for the evening dinner, they apparently discussed what was and might be going on at the high school. They also discussed the use of their church on Saturdays.

Late in the afternoon the pastor stopped by the church to see how things were coming. One of the ladies, the wife of a leading member, told him that they had been discussing the Saturday program and had come to the conclusion that it ought to be stopped. When the surprised minister asked why, he was told that "the people are convinced that sooner or later serious damage will be done to our church."

After the worship service two days later, the pastor asked all members of the church board to stay for a special meeting. He reported that he had received some opposition to the Saturday afternoon program and said that he had called the meeting to let them reaffirm their support for this ministry. He reported briefly on the success of this endeavor.

When he concluded, there was a long silence. Finally, one of the men said, "Reverend, it just won't do for us to have that group of kids in the building. They will wreck this place."

The discussion continued for several minutes, with the members of the board voicing their objections and the pastor defending the program. Finally someone suggested that they take a vote on whether or not to permit the group to meet in the church building. Eleven persons voted no; only one person voted yes.

The pastor was disappointed, but he did not feel that the decision was crucial. Bethany, the largest church on his circuit, was only two miles away. When he was planning the Saturday afternoon activity, he had considered having it in that church because the facilities were better. The Bethany members were enthusiastic about the idea. He had selected Shady Grove because of its more convenient location to the Indian children. He now planned to move the program to Bethany.

The next Saturday the children were taken to Bethany Church. Those who walked to Shady Grove were picked up at the church and driven to Bethany. The usual number of children attended. However, the following Saturday the attendance dropped sharply. Instead of over fifty Indian children, only eight came. There was also a drop in the number of mill workers' children. Two weeks later the program had to be discontinued because almost no one would come.

Questions for Discussion

What was the connection between the racial incident in the high school and the sudden objection to the program for the Indian and mill workers' children in the Shady Grove church? The pastor did not anticipate a negative reaction by the children and possibly their parents when he moved the program to a different church. How do you account for the fact that the children stopped attending? How might the minister have won the support of the Shady Grove members? Given the current situation, what might be done to improve relationships among the members of these three groups (the Shady Grove members, the mill workers, and the Indians)?

VI   Examining Local Church Mergers and Relocations

All change involves threat, loss, and death.

It is not difficult to understand how change involves threat. What gives us a sense of well-being and security is a general environment which supports us. This may be an interpersonal environment, a social environment, an institutional environment, or a theological environment. The supportive environment of the "old" church location, group membership, and theology gives one a tremendous sense of security. To suggest or to provoke change is to introduce a restructuring process at all levels of experience and to alter the support structures people have come to see as dependable. Thus, to plan either a local church merger or a relocation is to introduce a significant threat to a congregation.

The threat and conflict produced cannot be resolved by rational arguments alone. Emotions, tradition, home, aspiration, and vital group membership patterns are being affected. Discussions couched in fiscal, logistical, and ministry-in-the-abstract rationales cannot carry the day against the negative feelings evoked by the threat of actually terminating one congregation's life and relocating the remnant. It may make all the sense in the world to merge, but wars have been declared and independence won in the face of what did not make sense! Attention must be given to both the life of the congregation "as is" and the reasonableness of change.

It was not reasonable for God to send his Son or the eleven disciples of Jesus to press on after the betrayal and death of their leader. In a very profound sense Christianity itself gains its strength and uniqueness from what seems unreasonable. This theological motif is released, as well as one's emotional involvement in the present church, when discussion and rationale for merger are presented. The emotional and theological commitment to persist despite overwhelming odds cannot be underestimated at any level of analysis in our effort to understand the conflict involved in mergers and relocations.

The loss associated with a potential or actual merger or relocation is sensed deeply and stirs feelings of sorrow and grief. These go well beyond the direct loss of a physical building. The feeling of loss of "place" applies not only to geographic place but to personal place, group place, memory place, and ministry place. The appropriate sense of "place" which accumulates over a period of years simply cannot be transferred and transplanted. It dies and a new "place" and sense of belonging must be developed; they cannot be relocated.

Death is an experience which transcends the physical death of a human being or beloved pet. Death is a continuous process. All activities and processes eventually die. The significant differences among deaths lie in terms and conditions of the experiences and activities involved. The universality of death does not impel us toward morbidity. Our awareness of the relative degrees and kinds of death brings us to the ultimate conclusion of death: potential and new life. When change threatens imminent death, we tend to become preoccupied with loss and are unable to consider the potential for life flowing out of death. Despite formal attempts to emphasize a "new life–new place" dimension of local church merger and relocation, the congregation finds the logic of the proposal overpowered by the encompassing experience of loss and death. No argument about potential benefits to be realized from merger or relocation, regardless of how convincing, can offset the immediate sense of death associated directly with the change, potential or actual.

As human beings we are conservative creatures when it comes to change. We tend to see the strength of the actual place and experience of our environment despite its many weaknesses and disadvantages. This is a known, whereas change introduces the unknown—the imminent prospect of having to begin a new life after the death of merger or relocation. That prospect can make the preservation of the *status quo* compelling and reveal the strength that can be summoned to resist change.

We may be strongly motivated to accept and initiate change because of overwhelmingly negative associations with our actual situation. In this instance we are willing to gamble that the life after the death of change cannot be worse, so we have little to lose. But ultimately we must confront the conflict between the potential attractiveness of change and what we give up and what must die before the new can become alive. If a group rushes headlong into change, ultimately the death in the merger or relocation acquires a destructive and not a constructive force.

So in contemplating and planning merger or relocation we need to acknowledge the strength of the loss and the threat reactions inevitably generated by such discussion. Fruitful conversation and plans will need to balance the loss against potential gain. Such gain can be perceived not in absolute terms, but only in potential and tentative terms. That is, the focus for the life after death aspect of the merger should be cast in terms of developing the potential to regain or reinvest in alternative and viable forms of ministry the commitments and investments in what is currently going on.

An important dimension of the reinvestment program is ministry to the congregation itself. Certainly that is a viable and necessary form of ministry. To pitch the argument for relocation only in terms of what the new group can do for the community and those outside the church, without open and practical concern for resolving the conflicting feelings of death and loss in the group being merged or relocated, is to abdicate an essential ministry to the bereaved church members. Reinvestment of energy occurs slowly. The grief process cannot be rushed by neglect, although it can be facilitated by active participation.

Merging Should Be Easy

Mt. Zion is a small rural church located in a county which has been losing population. It is the smallest congregation on a four-point circuit. In this case, an entire church group actively became involved in discussing and trying to determine its own destiny. In some ways this makes the final resolution easier because ultimately it is a group decision. But opinions and convictions are far from unanimous. The pastor has to consider his own mixed feelings as well as those expressed, directly and indirectly, by laymen in the church. The pastor, Mr. Raymond, tells us:

Mt. Zion is the weakest church on the four-church circuit of which I am pastor. The membership roll lists seventy-one members, but it is certainly not up to date. Probably fifty can be accounted for, and several of these are unable to attend church because of age or ill health. Others simply cannot be motivated to attend services.

There are two worship services a month—one at 10:00 A.M. on the first Sunday and the other at 7:00 P.M. on the third Sunday. About twenty-five persons attend the morning service and about twelve the night service.

The church school probably reveals more about the life of the church than do the worship services. It has been the church school that has kept the church going. There are three classes at present: preschool through second grade with five enrolled; third through sixth grade with eight enrolled; and the adult class with fifteen members. There are twenty-eight enrolled with an average attendance of twenty. Several of the adult class members are actually members of another church. The church school superintendent (who does an excellent job) is a member of the Episcopal Church.

When I was appointed to this charge three years ago, it seemed the church would be forced to close. Only one person was at the first worship service. She voiced a fear of the church's closing and said she would do anything to keep it open. At the next worship service there were five or six present, and we discussed the possible future of the congregation. They were elderly people and were determined to continue church services. I promised them that as long as they wanted to have services, I would be there and would do what I could to motivate interest. From that they went to work encouraging others to support the church. Slowly (over a year's time) the attendance increased. Some church families came back after they realized the church might pull through. The church was able to pay its obligations (except the denominational benevolences), paint the church, and buy new hymnals. Two new families were added to the membership. One family had two children, the other four. In general, the church has made progress, even raising the pastor's salary the next year and paying conference benevolences this year. But this is where my problem begins.

I have been encouraging merger with another church on the charge—one is five miles away and the other is seven. However, the five or six elderly persons who endured those first few months to keep the church from closing are opposed to this. The middle-aged and young adult leaders are giving serious consideration to merger.

The lay leader, a middle-aged man, approached me concerning merger saying he thought it would be in the best interest of all because he saw a need for a fuller church program and especially more worship services. However, he has repeatedly said, "It would send my mother to the grave to see it close."

The chairman of the stewardship committee, a man in his mid-thirties with four children, has asked about merger many times. But he always concludes, "Of course my mother-in-law would not go along with it."

Being realistic, I think merger would be best, but I have also emphasized that the members should let the church have a "dignified death," that is, plan its closing.

Questions for Discussion

The pastor made a commitment to the five or six faithful members that he would keep the church open while he was pastor. In the light of the probable lack of growth potential, should he honor this promise? Can the pastor talk to the younger members about a possible merger without the older persons feeling that he has betrayed them? Given the present situation, what course of action should the pastor and laymen follow?

Resurrected Before Its Time

Reasonable criteria for closing or merging a church seem self-evident. In our more circumspect moments when we are able to pull away from a close involvement in a particular church situation, we sigh and say, "Yes, that church really should close for its own good. Upkeep costs are too great, and the programs are too limited to be of any significant value, especially for the children. There's simply no growth potential in the community. It's really not worth the effort."

But then, lo and behold, we find ourselves in the situation of the Reverend Jerry James. As a pastor who is ministering to a small and supposedly dying church, Jerry can see both sides of the conflict. He sees the strength of Bethany; yet on a larger scale he is aware of the historical, cultural, and logistical problems which continue to press in upon the church. These sometimes appear insurmountable. Jerry describes his dilemma as follows:

The smaller of the two churches (Bethany) has only a few people in attendance on Sundays. Some days there are only eight or nine there.

Records are scanty, but indications are that this church has been put out to pasture by at least the past two pastors. The previous two pastors served a total of six years. They simply went through the motions of ministering while waiting for the church to die a natural death. Bethany has been a grand worship center in the past, but even the members spoke of it as being in times gone by. When I came, the church had nineteen members on the rolls. There were only six families. Two of these families have quit coming. One daughter married a Jehovah's Witness, and the father of the other returned to drinking very heavily. This leaves only four of the original six families in attendance.

In spite of this history, however, about eighteen to twenty-seven persons attend Bethany each preaching Sunday. Half are under twenty-five years of age. These people, who were giving nothing last year, paid $134 toward the benevolence program. They have built and paid for a new porch on the front of the building. All in all, the church took in more money last year than in the past several years. I realize that money is not a criterion for judging the success of a church, but I feel it is an indication of how things are going. They now have enough money in the treasury to get the church painted. They have also agreed to accept a larger portion of the charge budget for the coming year.

Things would appear to be looking up. However, the country is very poor, and there are few people to draw from the area. Almost everyone in the immediate area has been aware of the failing condition of this church. They are not likely to come to it. The young people are reluctant to join for the same reason. In the long run, this church seems ultimately headed for the grave.

My problem is that I am beginning to feel guilty about the shot in the arm Bethany has received under my ministry. I feel like a doctor who has given a man a shot only to prolong his life for another day or so. Have I done these people an injustice by prolonging that which seems to be inevitable? What should a person do who has such a situation? Should he assume the position of the two preceding pastors, and simply go through the motions until the Bethany church dies? Or should he try to rebuild that which can be salvaged?

There is hope. But is this a genuine resurrection, or is it a kind of last gasp before death?

Questions for Discussion

In a situation in which there seems to be so much strength and weakness, what do you accept as evidence for acting either to build a new church or to close the old one? Does this situation call for a rethinking of the basic goals of the local congregation? As pastor, how would you try to resolve Mr. James's dilemma? If you were a layman in this congregation, what do you think your reaction would be?

To Relocate—or Not Relocate

First Methodist Church is located in an old residential community four blocks from the central business district in an industrial city of 75,000. The city has been growing, mainly to north and northeast. A mountain on the south has prevented expansion in that direction.

The membership of First Church is 1,200. This represents an increase of 200 in the past five years. The church building occupies all the available land. No off-street parking is available. The parsonage is across the street from the church.

The church building was constructed in two stages. The sanctuary was built in 1868. This consists of a fellowship hall on street level and a sanctuary on the second floor. The educational unit, erected in 1928, is three stories and contains a gymnasium, the only such facility in a church in the city. This part of the building is structurally sound. However, an engineering study has revealed serious structural problems with the sanctuary unit which will necessitate replacement or extensive repairs.

Seven years ago First Church conducted a study to plan for the future of the congregation. As a result, it was decided to remain at the present site and to secure additional property for parking. It was decided to encourage the development of a new congregation in the growing northeastern section of the city.

The new congregation, Grace, was organized in a section approximately four miles from First Church. The denomination provided money for a first unit and the pastor's salary. Due to a particularly inept organizing pastor, the new congregation did not do well for several years. Now in its sixth year and third pastor, the church has 150 members and still receives some subsidy. However, it is in a growing area and promises to be self-supporting in a year or two.

Three years ago First Church discovered that it was impossible to secure any adjacent land for parking. Consequently, attention turned to the possibility of relocating. A tract of land approximately two miles due north was available. The owner would sell it only to a church. The congregation purchased this property without having definite plans or a time schedule for relocation. A successful financial campaign was conducted to raise money to purchase land. Sufficient pledges were secured to enable the proposed site to be debt free in one more year.

In the three years since the property was purchased, some church members have begun to have doubts concerning the wisdom of relocating. Some feel that the proposed location is too close (a half mile) to the large Presbyterian church which had relocated out of the downtown area approximately nine years ago. Some members are questioning the wisdom of spending any money on building in the light of current mission needs. Others prefer to simply do nothing.

Others feel that First Church should remain downtown in order to provide a central city ministry. Members who favor relocation point out that nine other congregations are in or near the central city area. These include a strong United Church of Christ and an Episcopal congregation.

Opposition to First Church's proposed relocation has come from the pastor and some lay members of Grace Church. They feel that having First erect a new building approximately two miles west of their church will mean competition which will prevent the growth of Grace's membership.

The senior pastor has attempted to remain neutral, although privately he favors relocation. He is convinced that a move to the new site would enable the church to serve a larger group of persons more effectively. He feels, however, that the decision should be made by the laymen. The associate pastor strongly favors the present location and has circulated a mimeographed paper urging that First Church remain at its present site. His argument is that a mission to the central city is needed and this can best be performed at the present location. The associate pastor is a close friend and classmate of the pastor of Grace, who opposes the relocation of First Church.

The senior pastor has not discussed with his associate either their differing views on the relocation or the role the pastors should play in this decision. He has not indicated his displeasure with his associate's actions, although he feels strongly that the associate acted most unwisely.

There is evidence that the congregation is being polarized between those who favor relocation and those who do not. A significant proportion of the younger members favor relocation. Those who prefer to have the church remain downtown seem to be two groups, those who would have an active central city mission program and those who would simple preserve the status quo.

Questions for Discussion

The congregation of First Church has come to an impasse concerning whether or not to relocate. The polarization of the congregation is symbolized by the conflicting opinions of the pastors. What factors should be considered in determining whether First Church should relocate or remain at its present site? How much importance should be given to each? What will be the probable effect on the congregation if the church moves? If it stays? How should the decision be made? How will difference of opinion of the pastors affect their relationship to each other? To the congregation? What action should be taken? By whom?

VII   Encountering
Ecumenical Conflict

Ecumenical conflict is a phenomenon rarely experienced by the average local congregation. There are several reasons which explain this. We have been living in an era of ecumenical good feeling, at least good feeling among the major Protestant (and to some degree the Roman Catholic) denominations. The emphasis on the things which the different religious groups have in common has made an unecumenical utterance or action almost synonymous with the unforgivable sin.

While the leaders have proclaimed the oneness of the church, the local congregations have continued to operate in much the same manner—as autonomous units within their community subject primarily to the wishes of their members and whatever control their denomination desires or is able to exert.

Local congregations tend to come together in certain formal ways or to engage in projects which unite them in pursuit of a common goal. An example of the former is the community-wide Thanksgiving Day service in which all the pastors participate and which rotates between the different churches. An example of the latter would be several churches engaging in a campaign for some desirable civic or humanitarian goal. In such cases the goal for which the churches are working or the enemy that they are striving to defeat provides the unity and minimizes the likelihood of controversy. Furthermore, any of the participating groups can simply withdraw should they desire to do so.

There are, of course, some church groups which do not share in this era of ecumenical good feeling. They have as one of their tenets the apostasy of the mainline denominations. The leaders of such churches tend to attack the larger denominations. The main effect is to create solidarity within their own group. Attacks are usually ignored by the major Protestant denominations, who do not deem them worthy of an answer. While such groups have proved worrisome in certain local situations to the mainline denominations who do sometimes lose members, they are not seen as a major threat.

This is not to say that there is no conflict between churches of different major denominations. Rather it is to say that the local congregations have such limited contact with each other, particularly in those areas where the individuals' lives are significantly touched, that there is little opportunity for conflict.

Conflict tends to occur at three points. The first is when churches of more than one denomination, each with a somewhat different idea of the mission of the church, engage in a joint effort at ministry. For example, two churches attempting to minister to migrant workers discovered that they had an entirely different concept of ministry. One group placed a high priority on evangelistic services; the other thought that the major effort should go into a recreation program for the migrant children.

A second point of potential conflict is when churches of different denominations attempt to work closely together in some form of cooperative parish. Many of these are in rural areas where the individual congregations do not have sufficient strength to maintain their own church. In such cases the institutions are brought into a close relationship in areas that touch the lives of the members. Cherished institutions with a long history may be threatened. Conflict is not uncommon.

A third type of ecumenical conflict is between denominational administrators. Few laymen and pastors are aware of this conflict because they are not personally involved and because such rarely gets publicized. This controversy may be between denominations over such matters as which one shall organize the new church in a rapidly developing suburban community, one with a potential population large enough for only one congregation. Ecumenical conflict also occurs within interdenominational organizations such as councils of churches. Bitter battles have been fought over certain denominationally funded but ecumenically operated ministries. Unless the program is particularly controversial and gets publicity in the secular press, such conflict is known to only a very small number of persons.

The Consultation on Church Union (COCU) has not caused a particularly high degree of controversy because it has not affected the local churches in any significant way. There are, of course, some individuals who are simply against it, but most people apparently do not have any strong feelings about the subject. Discussions have continued on the denominational and theoretical levels with not much concern in the local congregation.

In the unlikely event that an attempt is made to implement the present parish plan designed by the Consultation on Church Union, the level of controversy in the local congregations would reach a height unknown in modern times. This plan calls for the combining of several congregations into a parish so designed that it will include a range of racial, social, and economic groups. This proposed parish structure would threaten the local church and the individual's role in it. Furthermore, it would bring together a highly diverse group of people in an organization which did not evolve from the experience of the participants but which was imposed from outside. Such a situation could hardly be more ripe for conflict.

This chapter will present three cases involving conflict between mainline Protestant groups. These include controversy over a program and youth worker sponsored by several churches, a disagreement concerning an attempt to merge three rural congregations representing two denominations, and a conflict over the organizing of a new church desired by laymen but opposed by their denominational executive.

Don't Step on the Ecumenical Banana Peel

A great amount of discussion concerning the value of cooperative and ecumenical ministries has surfaced recently. Typically, interest is expressed in having several small churches join forces in much of their programming and administrative life. This could result in considerable financial savings through a common administrative center. Secretarial services could be concentrated and accomplished by one person, and so on. This would free the pastor of the small church to invest more of his time in ministerial duties.

Correspondingly, combining various programs such as vacation Bible school, day camp, day care, and other community-oriented projects would be feasible on a scale and with an effectiveness not possible within the limited resources of a single church. The real problem comes in staffing. Ministers can be encouraged to support and develop such cooperative projects in principle. But when it comes to the actual day-to-day administration and participation in such a ministry, an added dimension is introduced. No one minister wants to lose his personal autonomy or the historical integrity and tradition of his congregation.

The following problem is presented by Mr. John Nova, who was recruited to work in the Concord parish, a new cooperative ecumenical ministry of nine churches within a three-mile area. Originally, great hopes were expressed for this group. John sensed the enthusiasm of the ministers and their plans and dreams for what the Concord cooperative parish could accomplish.

John was not assigned to a particular parish. He was a specialist in youth work. He was not to be identified as the pastor of any particular church but would work to develop youth activities and programs for all nine churches. The laymen saw him in this light and graciously accepted him. The Bible school, the day camp, the day care work, and the junior and senior high programs, which John worked diligently to establish on an ecumenical basis, all prospered. John was extremely gratified by the support and morale of the participants in this very complicated arrangement.

The beginnings of John's problems were not intrinsic to what he was doing. Within two months of John's stay, some of the parish brethren began to express their doubts about the Concord parish. John was doing well—too well, in fact! As an outsider he had come in and established in short order a highly visible and enviable youth program. Some of the pastors had been singularly unsuccessful in developing similar programs, either cooperatively or in their own parishes. They saw John gaining too much credit as an outsider and as one who, according to critics, was not a parish minister in the true sense of the word.

The two churches which were most instrumental in designing the ecumenical ministry were quite conservative theologically. They had experienced some difficulty in holding their young people in church-based programs. But as John, the energetic outsider who was also liberal, began to develop a strong program, these two churches which had initiated the movement wanted out. The battle cries of the liberals and conservatives soon could be heard above the call to leadership and mission. The divisiveness became apparent to all, including the young people who had so warmly received John and the ecumenical programs he built.

In the final analysis, John claimed that as each pastor and parish saw their own autonomy threatened by the ecumenical movement, each was eager to pull out and abandon the project. Eventually the whole cooperative ministry fell into disrepair and was disbanded.

Questions for Discussion

Would it be correct to say that the Concord Cooperative Parish was conceived out of administrative and programmatic considerations and not theological convictions, so that as soon as issues came close to home theologically, the various parties were convinced that they had much more to lose than to gain?

When debating, discussing, and developing ecumenical projects, how much serious consideration is given to understanding the depth of personal, theological, and congregational threat involved?

Someone has said that the emotion of anger is an aggressive way of pushing a threat away from us; thus, one of the primary considerations in trying to develop any ecumenical and cooperative ministry would be the need for an open assessment of the degree to which such a ministry would be threatening to all concerned. Do we include such basic considerations in our plans?

We'll Go Our Own Way

Williamston is a small village of less than 200 persons located in a predominantly rural section of the south. The population of both the village and the surrounding area has remained relatively stable for at least twenty years. There are no indications that any drastic changes will take place in the community in the near future. The village contains a store, a garage, a post office, a school, a combination fire station and municipal building, and a Presbyterian church. Two Methodist churches are located outside the village, one approximately a mile north and the other approximately a mile and a half south.

These churches were served by two full-time pastors. The Presbyterian minister is a young man serving his first congregation after graduating from theological seminary. He lives in the manse located about a block from the church.

The Methodist pastor came into the ministry late in life. He had owned a small business which he sold in order to enter the ministry when he was in his mid-fifties. He is not ordained but serves as a full-time lay pastor.

The Presbyterian church has a membership of 131 persons. Williams Chapel, the Methodist church located about a mile and a half to the south of the city, has a membership of 81. Bethel, the church north of the village, has a membership of 52. Both Methodist churches have adjacent cemeteries.

At a state meeting of denominational executives, the

Methodist and Presbyterian administrators who had responsibility for the churches in Williamston fell into conversation about their work in that area. They discovered that each of the pastors was being supported by denominational mission funds. The Presbyterian church was receiving an annual subsidy of $5,000 toward the pastor's salary; the Methodist churches were receiving a total of $3,250 per year, also used to supplement the amount the congregations paid the minister.

The two denominational executives raised the question with each other of whether it was good stewardship of their resources to allocate $8,250 toward the support of the two pastors serving three churches which had a combined membership of 264. The two men quickly agreed that it was not. They decided that they should do something about it.

Their first step was to meet with the pastors of the churches to see whether they were interested in working out some kind of cooperative program. The Presbyterian minister was highly enthusiastic about the prospect. The Methodist man was not enthusiastic but did not appear to object.

The next step was to call a meeting of the congregations to discuss the matter. This was done, apparently with a high degree of success. The visiting executives and the pastors decided in advance that they would say little except to present the subject for discussion. They would let the laymen express their feelings. At the onset a Presbyterian layman made a statement saying that he was a former Methodist who had married a Presbyterian girl, and that he hoped they could work together for a more effective ministry in the community. This was followed by a Methodist lady who expressed her concern about the small number of children in the Sunday school. She indicated that her eight-year-old daughter had only one other girl of her own age in her Sunday school class. She said, "You simply can't have a good Sunday school class with two children; I hope we can work together so that we can do a decent job with the education of our children." Similar comment followed. There were no negative speeches. The meeting ended with the appointment of a committee to work on the details of a cooperative program.

This committee did its work speedily and apparently well. The three churches would function as a parish. It was decided to combine the Sunday schools, using the Presbyterian facilities. This church had a small but adequate educational unit with individual classrooms. The other churches had limited church school space. It was also decided to rotate the worship services among the three participating churches, having the service in a different church every Sunday.

The people were told that the denominations could not afford to continue the high level of subsidy and that only one pastor would be available to serve the three churches. The Methodist congregations agreed to accept the Presbyterian minister as their pastor, and the Methodist minister was assigned to another church at the session of the annual conference.

The beginning of this venture seemed almost too good

to be true. It was. Within three months dissatisfaction began to be heard. The Methodist parsonage, an eight-year-old house adjacent to Williams Chapel, was vacant. There were complaints by some Methodists that they had erected a large and expensive parsonage which now was standing empty and going to ruin. The rotation of the worship services proved to be a point of growing contention. There was confusion as to where the preaching was to be held. Some complained that there was confusion which was preventing people from attending. Another complaint was that the subsidy had been reduced, but the local budget was as high as ever.

Six months after the initial meeting and three months after the Methodist pastor had moved out of the community, the Williams Chapel people decided to withdraw from the cooperative parish. A group of the members met at the church and made the decision. They notified the Methodist administrator by letter that they would "no longer participate in or contribute to the parish." They expressed their appreciation for the Presbyterian pastor, but indicated that "a church which has served for 128 years should not be allowed to die." They were convinced that their continued participation in the parish would lead to this.

They also indicated that if the denomination did not send in a pastor they would make other arrangements. A pentecostal lay preacher living in the area had already agreed to hold services. He was scheduled to begin in two weeks. A copy of the letter was sent to the Presbyterian pastor.

Questions for Discussion

What appeared to be an ideal ecumenical parish seemed to come apart almost before it got started. Given the fact that the Williams Chapel people seem determined to withdraw, what might the pastor do? What should be the stance of the Methodist executive?

The initiative for this parish came from outside the congregations. Furthermore, the plan was implemented in a short time. How might this have affected the rejection by one of the churches before the plan had time to be adequately tried? What now would be the best way for the people of the Williamston churches to carry on an effective ministry?

Let's Get This Church Organized

Riverview is a developing community on the edge of a large midwestern city. The growth of this section of the metropolitan area is limited because of the river's western shore, which is low ground that occasionally floods.

As the Riverview community began to develop, a local council of churches staff member studied the area and its potential growth. He decided that the population would be large enough to warrant the establishment of only one Protestant congregation in the community. The Comity Committee, the group within the council of churches that assigned such communities to the participating denominations, discussed the matter and unanimously agreed that the United Church of Christ would be given the responsibility of providing a church for the Riverview area.

In due course this denomination secured a site, appointed a pastor, and organized a congregation. A small first unit consisting of a fellowship hall, four classrooms, and a church office was erected. This was financed through a combination of a grant and a loan from the denomination's mission society. The membership did not increase as had been anticipated. The pastor was young and relatively inexperienced. Some tension developed between him and several of the most active laymen. The result was that at the end of the second year the congregation still had only 109 members and still required a subsidy from the mission society to continue in operation.

About this time Edward Hanson, who had been a Methodist lay speaker at a church in Dallas, Texas, moved into the community. When he discovered that there was not a Methodist church there, he decided to remedy the situation. During the next three months he managed to locate a number of families who had been members of a Methodist church prior to their moving to the Riverview community. He talked with each of these about the possibility of their becoming the nucleus of a new Methodist congregation.

Mr. Hanson then called the Methodist district superintendent and asked if he would be willing to attend a meeting in his home to explore the possibility of a new Methodist congregation being organized in the Riverview section. Dr. Brown, the superintendent, was surprised and a bit embarrassed to receive this request. He told Mr. Hanson that under the comity agreement, the community had been assigned to the United Church of Christ, but that he would be happy to come out, meet with the people, and explain the situation. An evening ten days hence was agreed upon.

In the intervening days Mr. Hanson was determined to get a group together that would show the district superintendent that they were serious. He contacted all the former Methodists he knew and even put up a poster in the local shopping center inviting "all interested persons to attend a meeting concerning the organization of a Methodist church in Riverview."

One of the persons who saw the poster was the United Church pastor. He saw this as a serious threat to the possible growth of his congregation and as a violation of the agreement that no other church would build in the community. He called his denominational executive, who immediately called the Methodist district superintendent. Although the Methodist administrator explained that the coming meeting was called at the insistence of the local group and that his denomination had no plans to start a new church in Riverview, he did admit that he had felt somewhat angered that his colleague "virtually accused me of not abiding by the comity agreement."

The meeting was held in Mr. Hanson's family room. Thirty-seven persons attended. The room was packed; a number of people were sitting on the floor. Dr. Brown explained the comity agreement and how each denomination was assigned responsibility for different communities. He pointed out that the United Church had been given this community and urged those who wanted to be a part of a nearby congregation to join that church. Furthermore, there was a Methodist church about three and a half miles away.

Mr. Hanson had done his work well. The persons assembled were not to be easily dissuaded. One lady said she had been attending the United Church but dropped out because it was "a church full of tension where the people seem to be squabbling with the pastor." A man added that the United Church "doesn't have adequate facilities for a decent Sunday school."

Mr. Hanson pointed out that the group represented twenty-four families and that there were five other interested families who could not be present. These twenty-nine families represented ninety-six persons, including children. He said, "There are many Methodist churches with fewer members than that."

As a sensitive pastor, the district superintendent was reluctant to simply tell the group that the denomination would not, under any circumstances, found a new church in the community. Instead he complimented them for the effort they had put forth in getting the group together and for their enthusiasm. He promised them that the matter would be taken under advisement by the denomination and possibly by the Comity Committee. The people interpreted this as a positive response; the superintendent thought he had bought some time during which the enthusiasm might cool.

The word soon was out in the community that the

Methodists were going to start a new church. The United Church pastor heard this and phoned his denominational executive, who phoned the superintendent. The ensuing conversation probably did not do a great deal for ecumenical relations. It ended with the United Church executive more convinced that the Methodists were not keeping the comity agreement and the Methodist superintendent feeling that he could not abandon the group of lay people who wanted a church in their community.

Questions for Discussion

This case illustrates how an agreement in one level of the denomination can be frustrated on another. It further illustrates the local and volunteer nature of the church. Given the present set of circumstances, what would be the best course for the Methodist district superintendent to follow?

Would establishing a second church in the Riverview community be justified, particularly in light of the United Church's internal difficulties? What will be the response of the group of Methodist laymen if the denomination does not cooperate with them? What compromise solutions might be proposed?

VIII   Establishing Program
Goals

Establishing goals for any group involves four basic dimensions: (1) leadership style, (2) goal selection methods, (3) types of goals, and (4) developing priorities.

Leadership

There are two basic leadership styles: persuasive and reflective.[1] Both styles have their strengths and weaknesses. A "persuasive" style refers to the leader who advocates measures, goals, and programs which may at first appear radical. They may push his constituents beyond where they think they are and should be. A "reflective" style means that the leader gleans from his people the goals which are basically there but not yet clarified nor their implications recognized.

In the church, the pastor's or group leader's style will emerge in one of these two basic patterns. Any systematic analysis of the church's goals must consider leadership style. Once a basic style is identified, appropriate methods for establishing goals can be developed.

A third style may also be dominant. This would be

---

[1] Cf. Richard E. Neustadt, *Presidential Power* (New York: John Wiley & Sons, 1960), and Clinton Rossiter, *The American Presidency* (rev. ed.; New York: Harcourt and Brace, 1960).

the "default" style. Here the leader lacks a clear vision of what he or the group wants. Thus the line, or level, of least resistance is followed.

In any event, the leadership style greatly limits the effective methods for achieving goals.

Goal Selection Methods

The strong leader, whether a persuasive or reflective person, will help to initiate or clarify the group's goals.

In a democratic society consistent unanimity is simply not possible. Thus "group process" has surfaced in the church as an effective method of goal selection. Basically this is an extension of the reflective style of leadership. Here the group very self-consciously works out its goals while attempting to be attentive to the minority rights of those holding dissenting views. To be sure, small group process as an administrative method is far less developed and understood than it is as a therapeutic method. But we are interested in its administrative strength. And this remains to be fully realized in the church.

Corresponding to a default leadership style would be the "chaos" method of goal establishment. Here the person who talks the longest, has the largest lungs and the most insensitive ears emerges to establish goals by fiat. No one understands; everyone is confused; but all are happy that at least a decision was made, although chances are it is likely to come unglued between now and the next meeting.

Types of Goals

In the church the basic goals seem related to building construction, budget, membership, debt retirement, youth education, service projects, and recreation. One might ask, "Well, how about the worship of God? Isn't that a goal?" Having formal worship services is essential, yes. But actual worship occurs as a spontaneous expression. It is not a discrete program goal. To attempt to guarantee the worship of God would be to grant overt, objective behavior and action final authority. This approach would produce a cult of physical idol worship before long: what one sees, measures, and catalogs is omniscient and omnipotent.

General Motors or American Motors may say that making money is their goal. And the achievement of this goal can be established or discredited by objective means, such as units sold and after-taxes profits. The church cannot and may not capitulate to this kind of discrete goal.

As a community, the local congregation or national denomination establishes goals along the lines mentioned. The achievement of these goals can be more easily recognized in some areas than in others. Buildings, finances, and membership figures can be more readily determined than can educational, recreational, and interpersonal goals. But all are necessary types of goals in the church. The ultimate criterion for establishing goals is not the relative ease of describing them but the theological basis for redeeming and ministering to the whole man. And mankind needs shelter as well as the Lord's Supper, a devotional life, and group sensitivity.

Developing Priorities

Four main factors are involved in a church group developing priorities.

(1) Analysis. List the actual and possible goals involved and begin to derive a list of "options." What are the options theologically, sociologically, and personally?

(2) Debate. As options began to be compiled and commentary provided, the group or its representatives need to begin to discuss these options in order to select goals from the priorities acknowledged. If priorities are to be established, openness in debate must be guaranteed. No "kangaroo courts" here! Dissent and alternatives must be expressed and considered. A patterning of issues and priorities of issues will soon emerge from such a debate.

(3) Selection. Having proceeded this far, make the selection and stay with it. Much thought was required to bring the group to this point. Act with courage and alacrity. Be persistent and energetic—and this includes soliciting support from those originally opposing the goal. Give it a chance. If the opposition was correct, the effort will come to its own end. If criticism was wrong and the goal is being attained in a more profound way than anticipated, rejoice. But give it a chance. The next time the tides of judgment may run the other way.

(4) Reevaluation. A program may be doing well or poorly. In either case, routine evaluation and critical analysis is necessary in order to strengthen weak programs, cut back on ambitious ones (see the following case on the prerecorded youth program), and drop poor ones.

Goals cannot be established by organizational charts, colorful schematics, rip-roaring rhetoric, or computers alone. The church's goals are directly related to people. Their inception may be in lists and charts, but their achievement involves people, and this includes resolving conflicts over what the goals are and how they are to be achieved or reorganized. The following cases give some indication of the diversity and subtlety in establishing goals.

This Youth Program Is Prerecorded

Morris Miller is a young adult who was asked to be the adviser and counselor for the senior high group at Trinity Church. Being new in the community, he held high hopes for the group and for himself. But in their first encounter he found himself appalled by the group's apathy. This was a fruitless and frustrating effort to stir the youth to some responsive patterns; absolutely nothing happened.

After several days' reflection Morris decided to contact some of the youth, especially the officers, to try to discover the source of the problem. Was it him? Were the young people passively resisting him? He didn't think so, but he could not pinpoint what else the problem might be. So he began the rounds.

After several extended discussions the following situation began to emerge. There was nothing wrong with what the kids saw in Morris or with their willingness to work with him. But he had stepped into the middle of a long and simmering battle at Trinity between the adolescent children and their adolescent parents.

It seems that some years before, several creative and very energetic adult counselors hit upon a wonderful idea for the kids to make money for their group: the youth fellowship would sponsor a horse show! The kids were delighted at this prospect; what better way to combine their own interests with making money, satisfying their parents, and supporting the church and enjoying its praise? So it was.

Huge amounts of energy and planning went into that first year's horse show. Publicity. Food. Competitive events. Awards and gifts. Concessions of various types. It was an immense success. People from all over the county came. In a single year a tradition was established. But then the rub.

The manifest success of the show exceeded the dreams of both youth and parents. But the parents, not to be denied a good thing, sought to capitalize on their success. Shortly after the show, adults of the church began to lay plans for next year's show, to make it bigger and better. Nothing is intrinsically wrong with that. But the adults forgot, in their enthusiasm to create a bigger show and to make more money, to include the youth. In their adolescent greed the adults began to take over the horse show so that before long, Morris discovered, they were running the show almost exclusively while retaining the "youth fellowship" title. The young people were permitted token participation in such activities as running concession stands and clean-up operations. But the glory —well, that was reserved for the adults who wanted to extract maximum profit from this newly discovered gold mine.

The adults did turn over a percentage of the take to the youth. But they maintained and increased their control over the show. In their greed to institutionalize the horse show–gold mine they failed to see what they were doing to the youth, what they were saying about their own immaturity and greed—all in the name of church service for Trinity Church—and how terribly patronizing and exploitive all this had become.

"Prerecorded" indeed. Morris Miller now understood why he had been greeted with such overwhelming lethargy. This was a kind of reverse case of taxation without representation: profits without participation! The youth were more concerned about doing something well as a group than about making the most money possible in the shortest time possible. Morris set to work. He began to gain the youth's confidence as they outlined activities in which they wanted to participate, placed limits on the horse show, and developed new programs. Then they approached the adult adolescents.

Gradually the adults and parents began to see what

they had done to the youth and to themselves and how their esteem had been lowered, not raised, in the eyes of their children. Correspondingly, the youth began to show more interest in themselves and in the church as they, along with the adults, discovered that preprogrammed and prerecorded youth activities are nothing more than that: they are not human; they are not Christian; they are exploitive and vicious in their cycle. Success was not the basic goal the youth had for themselves and their church. And at Trinity they had fought against this attractive form of social cancer—unrestrained expansion—with the only means available: passive and apathetic resistance.

What was going on beneath the surface was not apathy and unconcern for church activities but quite the opposite: a deep concern for the integrity of Christian life so that the church must exercise restraint—even in its successful programs. Here the youth showed more maturity than their parents and other so-called adults in the church, and it took an outsider, Morris Miller, to discover this maturity and unleash this strength.

Questions for Discussion

So often we complain about the disinterest of young people in the life of the church, and this appeared to be the case at Trinity. How do we begin to establish communication within the church to go beyond appearances and discover what really is happening? What are the larger implications for the goals of the church when we consider that people's apathy may be the only way they have to protect their integrity from our compelling pre-occupation to make all programs and goals in the church bigger and better?

Buildings Aren't Everything

Building projects constitute very definite goals in themselves. But there is a great temptation to consider the completion of a new building an end in itself. Acquiring a building is only one portion of the overall goals which the church must keep in mind. Otherwise, there is a mixing of means and ends so that both pastor and congregation become confused about which is which. Evaluation of goals is difficult because building project goals are not kept separate from and subordinate to the ministerial goals of the church.

Paul Newcomb encountered this problem in his new United Methodist parish assignment. He was, however, aware of the need to establish and maintain differences between building and ministerial goals. But it was not easy. Here is his situation.

The group involved in this particular problem is a whole church congregation. The problem concerns whether or not an educational unit should be added to the present structure.

When I moved to this charge I was told that more than $5,000 had been raised in a six months' drive to build an educational unit. After a few weeks I began to ask questions about this project, wanting to become acquainted with the parish before any large projects were undertaken. This project seemed to be a sore spot with some members of the church. I asked about planning and learned that very little had been done in an organized effort to build. A building committee had been elected, but the chairman had moved away. There were no written records about plans.

Sometime later I began talking with my lay leader and some of the trustees regarding the situation. I learned that the congregation was greatly divided over this issue. I asked the building committee to meet with me. I learned that some were very passive in their attitude toward engaging in a building program. We tried to get someone to fill the vacancy created by the moving of the chairman. We were unsuccessful.

The attendance or the membership potential at the present time does not demand the addition of an educational unit. We have more than adequate space already. This is also the feeling of some of the members. However, what we do have needs to be renovated to make it really conducive to a learning situation in church school activities. We are not overcrowded in the least. Now the real problem lies in the question, do we build or not?

I have talked with both factions on an individual basis. Neither side will refute the other in administrative board meetings regarding this situation. Some say, "Let us go ahead and start; the money will come." We have $5,000 now, but it would take at least $50,000 to build. Others say, "We can't afford it, and anyway we don't need it."

In talking with the building committee, I told them that we would qualify for some institutional funds. I had talked with Dr. Williams, and he gave me some idea of procedures to follow. This approach did not go over too well. Their feeling of independence, which characterizes United Methodists throughout the county, really came through. Some did not want to build specifically to a code, and others felt they did not want anyone else involved. They mentioned the cost of the architect as being wasted money and offered other nonsense arguments.

The project has been idle now for over a year and is beginning to be a bone of contention with some. We have one lady who has called the shots for years who wanted to build but recently yielded to the group that wants to renovate. We have a few now that are creating some areas of division within the congregation. I'm sure that whatever is done, it will not meet with unanimous approval.

I have mixed emotions about the situation; but I have made it plain to both groups that I am willing to support any official commitment that the church may make—either to build or to renovate. I feel that both sides would like me to make their decision. The former minister made the decision to raise $5,000 in six months. I will be leaving at conference (eight months away). I do not know if the leadership in the congregation can handle such a project, or at least it hasn't been evidenced. Should I engage them in a few months' study and activity, including a community survey and so forth, so that they might be ready to say yes or no by the time a new minister arrives?

The people are wealthy but share very little with the church. We always meet the budget, but there is never any surplus that amounts to much.

Questions for Discussion

On the whole, Paul seems to be very conscientious about how to proceed, trying to get in touch with all the cross currents of feeling and commitment before pushing for definite resolutions. Is he too conservative at this point, or do you see this as the correct procedure? He comments: "I feel that both sides would like for me to make their decision." Should he come straight from the shoulder and tell the group where he stands on the issues and lead them in that direction? What do you make of his final, almost passing, comment, "The people are wealthy but share very little . . ."? How about the need to distinguish between ministerial and building goals in this light?

We Simply Don't Want To

When offered an appointment to Elm Street Church, the young pastor enthusiastically accepted. This was his first full-time church following graduation from the school of theology, although he had served as a student assistant during his last year in seminary.

Elm Street Church was just the kind of church he wanted. It was located in an older residential community not far from the downtown district of a midwestern city with a population of 68,000. The neighborhood had once been occupied by families who owned large, comfortable houses. But over the years considerable change had occurred. A number of the dwellings had been subdivided into two or more apartments. Some of the new residents were persons who had moved from the Appalachian Mountain regions of Kentucky and Tennessee.

Although the community was somewhat transient, it was still an attractive area, with treelined streets and fairly well maintained dwellings. The residents of the neighborhood in which the church is located are white.

Elm Street Church was never a large congregation. At its peak the membership was 376. The last decade saw a slow but steady decrease in members to the 289 currently reported.

Prior to his arrival the pastor was informed that the congregation had considered relocating but had rejected this course. He interpreted this as a desire on the part of the members to maintain a ministry to the community. He was somewhat surprised to learn that the decision to remain had been due to the fact that no suitable new location could be found! The denomination had already organized new congregations in sections of the city into which Elm Street Church might have moved. Furthermore, the members themselves lived in so many different parts of town that no site could be found that would be acceptable to a majority of them.

The new pastor also discovered that the activities of the church were designed for and participated in only by the members who now lived outside the neighborhood where the church was located. He felt very strongly that the congregation should have an outreach into its immediate community.

At this point a Scout official approached the minister to see if the congregation would permit newly organized troops to use the building. Two men who were members of another church were to serve as leaders. The pastor brought this request to the governing board. The members discussed the matter for an extended period, raising such questions as the financial cost to the congregation, the possible damage to church property, and the possible interference with church activities. However, the motion to grant the request finally passed with no negative votes.

The pastor subsequently pressed for more church programs designed for the residents of the immediate neighborhood. He suggested to the board that a door-to-door visitation be made to find unchurched families in the community. The response was that the people were too busy to undertake so ambitious a project.

A short time later the pastor suggested that the fellowship hall be opened one night a week as a kind of youth canteen or recreation center. He suggested that equipment such as ping-pong tables and possibly a pool table be secured. The response was that the current budget would not permit these items to be purchased. Several other suggestions brought the same response, polite interest, but there were compelling reasons why the suggestion could not be implemented.

At this point the pastor called in a representative of the denomination to consult with the board on the direction which the congregation might take. At a meeting with nineteen persons present, the question of the purpose of the church and its responsibility to the community was discussed. As the visitor pressed the members on just what it was they expected their church to be doing, it became increasingly evident that the situation was becoming more uncomfortable. The members simply did not want the residents of the nearby community in *their* church.

One lady with some indignation commented, "The year before last I spent a Sunday afternoon calling on people who live in this neighborhood, and do you know that we didn't get one of them to come to church. It was an entire afternoon wasted."

The minister kept pressing for a commitment by his board members to more programs aimed at the residents of the community. Finally, one of the most prominent members said, "I suppose this church really ought to be ministering to the people who live around here; but the plain truth is, we simply don't want to." There was a general consensus that this statement expressed the sentiment of the board members and the entire congregation.

On this note the meeting was adjourned.

Questions for Discussion

Prior to the meeting described above, the pastor did not sense the depth of opposition of his church to involvement with the residents of the community. Once these feelings were made clear, what should the minister do? What might he have done differently?

What do you think is the reason for the church members feeling so antagonistic toward the residents of the immediate neighborhood? Should the denominational officials intervene in this situation? If so, in what way?

Let Me Show You My Latest Plaything

Bob Sanders is an adult adviser for the senior high group at Four Seasons Church. His conflict over the leadership of the group grew out of an extended period of frustration.

Since November the youth fellowship had been trying to hold a retreat. Three times it had been cancelled. The first time involved another youth group. There had been a money-raising supper sponsored by both groups. But then discord occurred and each group went its own way. Their common kitty was not divided in time for Bob's group to finance its retreat. A second retreat was scheduled during the Christmas holidays. Bob and his wife, Sarah, had delayed some vacation travel plans in order to participate. But at the last minute Bob received a phone call from Eleanor, the other adult counselor. The president of the group, Becky, had decided to go to her sister's house at the beach instead of going on the retreat and had called all the youth and cancelled the retreat. Then Becky called the counselor, telling her to notify Bob. A third effort was scheduled for a weekend in February. In mid-January Becky again postponed it, this time until Easter weekend, because she had something else to do every weekend in February. In order to accommodate Becky, the group agreed to delay the retreat once again.

When the following conversation occurred, program plans had already been made and food donated for the February retreat. Those involved in this discussion are:

Eleanor, the other counselor; Henrietta, who is Becky's mother and Eleanor's aunt; and Bob.

Eleanor: Bob, about the retreat. Becky's not going to be able to go, and Betty and Rachel aren't sure if they're going either. But Jane, Doris, and Sandy are all planning to go. I wondered if you'd like to have it at your house since there are only three planning to come?

Henrietta: (laughing) You can't have a retreat with just three people.

Bob: Why not? That's half of our group. If I remember correctly, the same three plan to go this time who planned to go the last three times we've scheduled the retreat. I don't think we should call it off this time. (to Eleanor) I think that having it at our place is a good idea. The atmosphere will be different. Just let me check with Sarah (Bob's wife) to see if that will be convenient for her.

Eleanor: Good. Then I'll check with you and Sarah after church. I want to talk with you about the program anyway.

Bob: (Leaving) OK. I'll see you then.

Henrietta: But Becky can't go then. She's been invited to a senior party.

Bob: Well, I guess Becky will have to decide whether she wants to go to the party or the retreat. We agreed on this date almost a month ago, and this time I want everyone who wants to go to have the opportunity to choose to go. If Becky decides to go, she's welcome to come along. (Henrietta left without verbally responding, but her blank stare and her protruding lower lip gave her feelings away. Later, in church, she had nothing to say about the retreat, even though she was the chairman of the committee.)

Henrietta and Becky certainly seem to have a nice little plaything going in the youth fellowship. But in this encounter we see Bob and Eleanor taking steps to force them to resolve their conflicts. Becky and Henrietta will have to resolve their conflicts for themselves. They can no longer cajole the youth group into always changing their plans to suit the schedules of Becky and Henrietta.

Henrietta seemed to think it unfair to expect her daughter Becky to have to choose between a school dating party and a church retreat. What is being communicated to Bob, Eleanor, and the youth is that Becky's earlier commitment to a church-sponsored activity is not really important. So it seems that church work is something one does as entertainment or a peripheral activity when it is convenient. But if a significant event should come up in the meanwhile, why, of course it has priority!

The conflict was whether Bob and the group would continue to reinforce Becky's negative attitude and behavior. If the retreat were to be cancelled again, Becky would have conned others into capitulating to her whim. But, because the group went ahead with the retreat, Becky was forced to confront her own conflict: she would have to make a direct decision. And beyond that issue was the larger conflict. Bob and the youth fellowship in this action affirmed that Christian education is important.

Questions for Discussion

How often do we underestimate the significance and implications of changing plans and goals in the church simply to suit someone's convenience? What we have done was not to help the individual but to take away the constructive need for him or her to make his own choice, and by this kindly neglect we undercut the integrity of those who have sacrificed by making the decision to participate in a particular program with definite goals. How often have others had to pay sacrificially for changes we have made to suit our convenience? Do we really believe in what we plan? Did Becky? Or Henrietta?

IX Relating to Denominational Representatives

A point of potential conflict is between the local church and its denomination represented by an executive or a staff member of a board or agency. It is not an exaggeration to say that from time to time virtually every congregation experiences some degree of controversy with the communion of which it is a part.

The nature of denominational organization makes such conflict inevitable. One cause is that administrators and bureaucrats view the church with a different perspective than do local church members and pastors. Persons in such positions tend to see the denomination as a total unit. Thus, the regional administrator may have as one of his objectives the overall ministry in a given geographical area such as a county. Two congregations located in the same neighborhood may be perceived by him as an unnecessary duplication of services and a waste of ministerial manpower. The average member sees the church in terms of his local congregation. He may not think or care about many of the things that are primary concerns of the administrator. A nearby congregation of the same denomination may not be perceived by the layman as a problem as long as his church is progressing in what he feels is a satisfactory manner. This difference in perspective contributes to controversy.

Denominational agencies bring various types and degrees of pressure on the local congregation. Churches are asked to respond to a range of requests from their denomination. Foremost among these is to pay for the administrative overhead and to finance a wide range of mission and benevolent enterprises operated by church agencies. Local congregations are assessed a kind of voluntary tax to pay for this overhead and mission program. While most denominations do not spend an inordinate sum of money on administration and while most benevolence programs are worthwhile, they still require a considerable amount of funds. And no person likes to pay taxes, even voluntary ones. Even when the local people are generally in sympathy with the aims of such programs, they may resist the cost.

Furthermore, the assessments frequently come with a great deal of pressure from the denominational authorities. Such pressure is brought on the pastor whose success is at least partially determined by his congregation's willingness to pay the requested amount. The pastor may resent the fact that money which he would like to use locally is going to denominational activities. Thus the increase in denominational assessments may be perceived as jeopardizing the increase in the pastor's salary or the hiring of a parish visitor. The minister may resent the larger asking and pass on this feeling to his laymen.

Another source of conflict is the denominational programs which each local church is expected to follow. Such programs might include a simultaneous evangelistic campaign in every church or a denomination-wide study of some specific topic. While such undertakings may be worthwhile, they may also be resented as handed-down programs. Like the competition for funds, such programs compete for the time of both pastor and laymen.

A major cause of conflict between the local congregation and the denominational representatives is the difference in the ideological stance of the two groups. Controversy often is more intense over social issues than over theological issues. The persons in the denominational organizations in general tend to assume a more liberal stance, advocating certain social change which may be opposed by a portion of the local constituency. Because they are insulated from the laymen in the local congregation by the nature of their position, they can assume a less popular stand on controversial issues.

Furthermore, persons in the church bureaucracy tend to see their task as leading the denomination in the way that it ought to go (just as pastors see their task as leading the local congregation in the way that it ought to go). Because the bureaucrat has less immediate contact with his local clientele than does the pastor and because he is less responsive to the wishes of this constituency, the situation is ripe for conflict. There are times when the rank and file simply do not want to go in the direction that the official wants them to.

Pastors and people in the local congregation tend to distrust those persons employed as denominational administrators and staff members of boards and agencies. Ministers see such persons as having high salaried (correct), high status (partially correct), and easy (incorrect) jobs. They may not understand what such persons are attempting to do. Furthermore, they are "out there," a convenient scapegoat on which a variety of ills can be blamed.

Conversely, persons in the bureaucracy too often tend to assume an attitude of condescension toward the local congregation. In the rarefied atmosphere of the national office it is easy to feel that one knows what is best. This is illustrated by a conversation overheard in an elevator of a mission headquarters of a major denomination. Two persons employed in mission promotion were congratulating themselves on the success of a particular piece of literature which they had produced. They were judging this success by the number of complaints they were receiving from the people whom they were supposed to be convincing to support missionary projects!

In the conflict between the denominational representative and the local congregation, the pastor may find himself caught in the middle. He may be sympathetic with the goals of the larger body while sensitive to the feelings of his members. He is aware of the difficulties of making a denominational-wide program fit the particular congregation which he serves. Thus the pastor may find himself in the uncomfortable position of having conflicting loyalties.

There are indications that the amount of conflict between the church official and the local people is increasing. A successful ministry requires both the activities of the local church and the various denominational organizations. Destructive conflict between these can sharply reduce the overall effectiveness of the church.

Where Is Our Money Going?

The annual church conference was proceeding pretty much on schedule. The congregation had had a moderately good year. The budget had been met, and the treasurer reported that there would be a slight surplus when all outstanding bills were paid. The amount which the denomination had requested from Trinity Church toward the mission program had been met. The pastor had been invited to return for another year.

At the conclusion of the routine business the denominational superintendent, who was presiding, indicated that he had a matter to present. He reminded the persons present that their national denominational body had voted a large sum for special urban mission projects. Each congregation was expected to contribute toward this undertaking. When asked if they were aware of the action of their denomination, about a third of the members present raised their hands.

The superintendent talked at some length about the need for special ministries in the inner city. He mentioned the lack of opportunity for residents of the slums and described the decaying neighborhoods in which such persons live. He pointed out that their denomination had a special responsibility both because of the large number of city churches which they had and because of their size and strength. He indicated that one half of the funds collected from each local church would go to the national mission society to be used in whatever part of the country the need was greatest. The other half of the amount raised would be held for use in specific city mission projects in the local area.

The members of the congregation responded positively to this appeal by the superintendent. Even when he suggested the rather large amount of money which the congregation would be asked to contribute, there was no opposition. One layman, a business executive with considerable experience in the inner city area, spoke of the conditions there. He said that to minister in such communities was a challenge which the church should accept.

At this point a lady asked about the ministries this fund would support in the inner city. The response of the superintendent was somewhat evasive. An attorney in the congregation pushed the question a little harder, asking just what specific things the denomination would be doing in the old central city with which most of the members were familiar. The superintendent became visibly defensive and delivered a little homily, concluding by saying that the money "would be used to preach Christ to the residents of the ghetto."

The positive reaction of the members of the congregation began to change to negative as they sensed that they were not getting a clear response. A couple of more questions were similarly evaded. The meeting adjourned with a benediction by the pastor. The superintendent left somewhat hurriedly. The laymen stood around in little groups and discussed the failure of the denominational executive to give forthright answers. The pastor commented that the denominational committee which was to determine the local priorities for spending the money had not yet met. He indicated that the superintendent could not answer the questions because the decisions had not been reached.

This revelation by the pastor angered some of the members. One man commented, "Why didn't the superintendent tell us the truth? We could accept the fact that the decisions are pending."

A lady said, "It makes you wonder about our denomination's leaders."

"I'm not sure we ought to support this program," responded the chairman of the board of trustees.

"I'd just like to know where our money is going," commented his wife.

Questions for Discussion

This situation is one in which the seeds of mistrust and conflict were being sown. A potentially favorable response to a worthy undertaking was jeopardized. The congregation developed some degree of suspicion of their denominational executive.

Why do you think the superintendent was reluctant to tell the lay persons why he could not answer their specific questions? Was the negative reaction of the lay members to the superintendent justified? The pastor was aware of the real reason the superintendent could not answer the peoples' questions. Should the pastor have remained silent?

An Old Church and a New Community

The Bethel Church building was erected in 1911, although the congregation was founded in 1847. The present white frame building consists of a sanctuary which will seat 120 persons including eighteen in the choir. A fellowship hall and small kitchen are in the basement under the sanctuary. Four church school classrooms at the rear of the sanctuary were added in 1926.

For most of its existence Bethel Church has served a predominantly farming constituency, despite the fact that it is located only twenty-four miles from the center of a major city in the northeast. In the late 1960s, the erection of a new bridge and an expressway made the section where Bethel Church is located easily accessible to the central city.

With the opening of the expressway, a bus company established a new route and located its garage within a half mile of Bethel Church. The travel time by express bus to the central city is forty-five minutes. Three developers secured tracts of land near Bethel Church and began to erect houses in the middle price range. The area began to grow rapidly. The church is at the corner of one major development and across the highway from a second.

The church site is a little less than an acre. It is located on what was, before the construction of the expressway, the main highway. A neighborhood shopping center with eight stores has been constructed along the highway adjacent to the church property. It is probable that more commercial development will occur here.

Prior to the suburban development, the closest Protestant church was a small American Baptist congregation four miles away. Within a three-year period three other churches have been organized in the area. These include a Roman Catholic parish reflecting the outmovement of former residents of the ethnic neighborhoods of the central city, a fundamentalist Bible Presbyterian Church and a United Church of Christ. Indications are that the Roman Catholic Church and the United Church of Christ are prospering. Data were unavailable from the Bible Presbyterian Church. The Roman Catholic Church has erected a chapel, and the United Church of Christ has an educational unit and a fellowship hall. The Bible Presbyterian Church is meeting in a house.

Prior to the suburban development, the Bethel Methodist Church had an active membership of 91. It was served by a seminary student who lived in the nearby parsonage and commuted daily to a seminary in the central city. With the community growth, the congregation soon had 134 resident members. A full-time pastor with subsidy from the denominational minimum salary fund was appointed.

At this point the congregation began to discuss the question of whether to relocate or rebuild. It was impossible to secure additional land adjacent to the present location because the owner was holding it for possible business use. However, several well-located sites were available within a half mile of the church.

For several months the matter of a new church was discussed at length. At every board meeting a majority of the members strongly presented the reasons why the congregation could not undertake such a task. No formal decision was reached. The debate within the congregation subsided. Only 31 members were received during the year of debate while losses totaled 16, making the membership 149. A group of long-term members opposed to rebuilding or relocation were effectively blocking any action. Two families transferred to the United Church of Christ.

At this point the denominational official became actively involved in the situation. The executive of the mission society held several meetings with the pastor and the church officials. Data showing the potential growth of the community were presented, and the local church was urged to make plans to minister to the expected influx of people. The same group which effectively prevented action by the congregation opposed the suggestion of the denominational official. The congregation felt that the denominational official was trying to pressure them into an expensive building program.

The meetings in the main were cordial, but the majority of the congregation held firm. The question of the cost of a new building was a major objection. A strong attachment for the old building was evidenced. After several meetings and six months of effort, it became clear that the congregation was not going to act. At this point a seven-acre tract approximately a half mile from the present church became available. When presented with this possibility, the local church again affirmed the earlier decision to remain.

The mission society did not feel that it could delay further. It purchased the seven-acre tract, feeling that no better site for a church would be available. This land was then offered at no cost to Bethel if the congregation would relocate and erect a new building. Nevertheless, the majority of the members were still reluctant to leave the old building.

The matter was debated for several more months. The mission society felt that it could delay no longer. It presented to Bethel what was virtually an ultimatum. The congregation was told that it could relocate on the new site and erect a church which was adequate to minister to the growing community. If Bethel failed to do so, the denomination would send a second pastor into the community. A new congregation would be organized, and a new church erected on the seven-acre site. The present salary subsidy for the Bethel pastor would cease at the end of the year. The congregation was asked to reach a decision by the next regular meeting of the mission society, which was four weeks away.

Questions for Discussion

The conflict here involves more than the church. It is between the old community and the new. To what degree does the fact that the suburbanites are disrupting the old established community influence the decision of the congregation? Could there be an age or generation gap operative in this situation?

How should one's understanding of the church influence his action in this matter? What can a congregation do to help create community in a rapidly developing area? Did the mission society show adequate concern for both the old and new residents? Was the issuing of an ultimatum to the Bethel congregation justified? Would the establishing of a second congregation in the community be a wise course? To what degree should the wishes of the Bethel congregation be respected?

We Just Aren't Interested

Pine Hill County is in a predominantly rural section of the upper south. It is an area which had an emigration and population loss for over thirty years. The decrease in the number of inhabitants was reversed, however, during the past decade when the county experienced a very slight gain in the number of residents.

Nineteen Methodist churches are located in the county. Three are in the county seat, and three others are in towns. The remaining thirteen are either in the open country or in hamlets. Nine of these congregations have less than one hundred members, and four have fewer than fifty persons on the roll.

Four pastors serve these thirteen churches. Two pastors each serve a circuit of four churches, one man serves three, and another is pastor of two. Two of the circuits are self-supporting; the other two require subsidies from the denomination totaling $8,500 toward the ministers' salaries.

A new, aggressive superintendent has recently been appointed to the district in which Pine Hill County is located. He is most concerned about what he feels is the ineffectiveness of many small rural congregations. He has also expressed the opinion that much of the subsidy going into small churches only perpetuates weakness and is thus wasted.

After his first visit to the churches in the county, the district superintendent decided that something needed to be done about the rural churches. His first move was to call a meeting of the four pastors. The superintendent told the men that he wanted to learn more about their work, the problems of their churches, and how he might be of help.

The session was held at a restaurant in the county seat. Each man had a chance to tell about his church. The superintendent then talked at some length about his hopes for the churches. He stressed what he called the "inadequacy of the small church to have a well-balanced program," the need for "cooperation among the small congregations," and that "every pastoral appointment should not only be self-supporting but contribute to mission funds." He proposed that each of the churches participate in a self-study program to determine their long-term strategy and program.

This suggestion was not received by the pastors with any degree of enthusiasm. They agreed that there might be value in such an undertaking and agreed to ask several laymen from each of the churches to come to a meeting the following week. The superintendent then told the pastors that he had arranged for one of the staff persons in church planning from the denominational office to be present to give guidance on how the self-study would proceed.

As the members of the group were leaving, the pastor of the Stony Ridge circuit whispered to one of the other ministers, "He had already invited the planner. What would he have done if we had rejected the study proposal?"

The meeting was held the following Thursday evening. Every church except one had at least three persons present. The superintendent made an opening statement, saying that the purpose of the self-study was "to enable each congregation to be as effective as possible." He also said that the pastors were "wholehearted and enthusiastic in their support of the study program."

The staff person was introduced. He spoke about the details of the program, indicating that each church would be requested to gather information about its members, the Sunday school, the use of the building, the finances, and the community. When he had concluded this presentation, he asked if anyone had questions.

The first man to raise his hand was the lay leader of the Stony Ridge circuit. He began by saying, "It seems to me that we are being asked to do a lot of unnecessary work. Our church is getting along fine. We are doing the best we can."

Before anyone could answer, a man from Carter's Chapel, one of the smallest congregations in the county, said, "You just want to have our church merge with some other group. The last superintendent tried to make us merge with Bethel; he said we were too small to justify our existence. We aren't going to. Furthermore, do you realize that Carter's Chapel has produced two ministers in the past ten years?"

The superintendent tried to assure the group that he really did not have any preconceived plan, but it was clear that they were not convinced. He finally turned to one of the pastors and said, "We haven't heard from your ministers yet. Let's hear what they think." A long silence followed. Finally the pastor of the Bethel-Salem circuit said, "I expect that there will be some benefit to the churches."

The minister of the Stony Ridge circuit then said, "I don't see how this proposed church self-study will do enough good to justify the time it will take. We already have more information about our churches than we are using. I think we could better use our time visiting people and doing evangelistic work."

A lady commented, "It seems to me that this is just another program that someone working for the denomination has dreamed up and is now handing down to us. I don't see any need for it. I would like to suggest that we forget about this study or whatever it is."

A man sitting in the back of the room said forcefully, "I'd like to second that motion."

Questions for Discussion

The proposed study appears to have been rejected by the laymen and probably by the pastors. Do you think that the proposal for a self-study program by the thirteen churches was a good idea? Why did the laymen reject the self-study? Were the real issues discussed? What was the role of the pastors in this process? How did the timing of the proposed study affect its lack of acceptance?

What might the superintendent have done differently to get his plan accepted? Given the current situation, what might he do now?

Conflict

and

Resolution

A Case-Study Approach to Handling Parish Situations

Paul A. Mickey
and
Robert L. Wilson

Conflicts are inevitable in the process of growth, especially in the local church. Understanding the nature of these conflicts and how to grow through them is important to laity and clergy alike.

In this unique book, authentic case studies in which the authors or their associates have been involved are used to demonstrate the many types of conflicts which occur in the local church. Each chapter deals with a specific type of problem, ranging from proposed church mergers and relocations to differences in program goals, racial issues, and conflicts among members of the church staff. Discussion questions designed to stimulate constructive decision-making follow each chapter.

(continued on back flap)